THE CAPTIVITY SERIES:

The Key to Your Expected End

*"For I know the thoughts that I think toward you,
saith the Lord, thoughts of peace, and not of evil,*
to give you an Expected End."
Jeremiah 29:11 KJV

By

KATIE SOUZA

GET READY TO TRANSFORM
YOUR CAPTIVITY INTO PROMISE!!!

The Captivity Series: The Key to Your Expected End
is being described as
"THE BEST BOOK EVER WRITTEN FOR PRISONERS"

My prayer is for this book to be used by the Lord to show you how to enter into your created purpose while here on earth. Above all else, however, I pray that you realize your ultimate Expected End is to reign with Him forever (Revelation 22:5).
May you be strengthened in your journey on this pilgrimage in preparation for that glorious day!

ACKNOWLEDGEMENTS TO:

The Father of our Lord, Jesus Christ – Who, through loyal EEM partners, incredible staff, and selfless volunteers, has blessed this vision in countless ways. Thank You!

Mom and Dad for never giving up on me, loving me unconditionally, and supporting this ministry every step of the way.

My husband for putting up with me, cherishing me, and enabling me to make the dream happen.

Teresa Mozena (Manning) for partnering with me and believing in this mission from the beginning.

CONTENTS

HOW TO USE THIS BOOK

Throughout this study, God, by His Holy Spirit, is going to speak to you as He directly applies the Scriptures concerning ancient Israel's captivity to your present-day incarceration. In order to assist you in learning to recognize His voice, we have provided blank pages entitled Personal Journal Entries located at the back of the book. As you read through this study, God is going to put thoughts in your mind that will directly apply what you are reading to your captivity experience. On each page, I encourage you to highlight, underline and circle words or phrases that stand out to you. Then make Journal Entries at the back of the book on the thoughts the Holy Spirit gives you as you meditate on what you read. This practice will greatly aid you in developing your ability to hear from the Lord.

Through this same practice, I learned how to recognize God's voice, not only in Scripture, but within a personal relationship with Him. As He spoke and I obeyed, I experienced miraculous manifestations of His Presence throughout my entire captivity. He involved me in numerous supernatural healings, led the development of a ministry inside my prison, revealed to me my Expected End, led me in writing this study, and guided me in forming this present-day ministry.

The Lord even directed my family and me to appeal the 13-year sentence I'd been issued by the federal court, and because we obeyed the Lord's direction, the appeal was granted! Even more amazing was that six months **before** our victory the Father also told me what my new outdate would be. Sure enough, after I went to court and they recalculated my sentence, the date He gave me was exact! Later on, I will be talking in detail about all these events. Right now, I want you to understand that receiving specific direction from God is the result of building a relationship with Him and cultivating your ear to hear and obey His voice. The journaling process included in this study will greatly assist you in developing that connection with Him.

In Habakkuk 2, God commands us to make a written record of every revelation He gives us. Verses 2 and 3 say,

> *"...Write down the revelation and make it plain on tablets so that a herald may run with it. For the revelation awaits an appointed time; it speaks of the end and will not prove false..."*

As you read through this book, **actively listen for God's voice, journal every thought He brings to your mind, and always date your entries.** As time goes by you will see, as the Scripture says, that the things He tells you will not prove false, but will come to pass.

Be diligent in this and all that concerns Him,

Katie Souza

CHAPTER ONE

THE ARREST

"Therefore my people will go into exile for lack of understanding..."
Isaiah 5:13

Outside, I could hear my dog, Cotton, freaking out, which could only mean one thing: somebody undesirable was out there; so I stashed my gun in an accessible place and headed out the door. Stepping off the wooden steps, I felt the cold ground through the socks on my feet, reminding me that my boots were in the trash. The soles were melted because of the chemicals I was wading through. As I rounded the corner, there they were; the cops, with guns pulled, threatening to shoot my friend and the dog. At the sight of them, my stomach flipped.

Just the night before, we came up the mountain so I could cook a batch of speed. The house was a virtual toxic waste dump, knee-high in chemical trash left behind by a bunch of wannabe cooks. I spent all night trying to clean up the mess so I could get started, but now the cops were here. "If they go inside," I thought to myself, "we will go down for sure."

I tried to tackle Cotton but she was totally out of control, leaping and snapping at the police. It was obvious she was my dog because she hated uniforms just as much as I did. The cops, acting like they could read our minds, were drawn down ready to shoot; so I grabbed Cotton by the neck and put my body in front of her as a shield. "Don't kill her!" I screamed. "Let me put her in the house!"

But they didn't back off. They just kept yelling for me to step back so they could fire. When they finally realized I wasn't going to budge, they let my friend drag Cotton inside. Once the threat of the dog was gone, they started questioning me. "We're here to clean up the house," I said, telling half the truth.

This wasn't what they wanted to hear so they continued badgering me for about fifteen minutes more. Then, finally, getting nowhere, they tried a new approach. They demanded I go back inside and get the dog so they could take her to the pound. Instantly, I flared up and started arguing with them. Now they wouldn't budge, so I spun around and headed back into the house.

When I opened the door, they came up behind me and barged in. Within half an hour, after they got a look at all the chemicals, I was sitting on the dirt in the driveway cuffed. "Well, it can't get any worse than this," I mused. Wrong. Five minutes later, the feds pulled up. Then my other two friends pulled in. They were arrested too.

"They finally got me," I said to myself. Deep inside I felt this time they were going to keep me too. Sure, I'd been arrested plenty of times before. Mostly on gun charges: assault with a deadly weapon, shooting from a moving vehicle, extortion. I loved my guns and had done "collections" for years. Not many people expected a girl to come to their door, pull a gun and take everything they owned to pay a debt. Fueled by some internal rage, terrorizing was my favorite sport.

However, even though I'd been arrested numerous times before, I always seemed to avoid doing any major time. Witnesses disappearing or lack of evidence forced some of my cases to be dismissed, but this time was different. There was no lack of anything to convict me. I just knew I was not going anywhere but down. As I rolled this thought around in my mind, I felt a kind of desperation well up inside of me, along with the vomit coming up my throat.

The next thing I knew I was drifting in and out of consciousness as an ambulance took me to the hospital. I was suffering from severe chemical poisoning. As my eyes would flutter open and close, I would always see one face before me: that of a federal agent, my personal escort. Once at the hospital, the doctors kept asking me questions I could barely understand, much less respond to. I was in such bad shape I continued to fall in and out of consciousness for many hours while they worked on me.

As night approached and I was deep in dreamland I heard someone say, "We need to go." Struggling to open my eyes, I saw the face of the federal agent as he gently tried to shake me awake. "You need to get up soon and get dressed." He said, as he unhooked my handcuffs. Hearing this, I closed my eyes for a few minutes wishing he and the reality that came with him would go away. When I reopened my eyes I realized my wish came true. He was gone!

I felt my wrists – no cuffs! Quickly I sat up, slid off the gurney and pulled on my clothes. Then, peeking out of the closed curtain, I saw the agent standing about 10 feet away at the nurses' station with his back toward me, deeply engaged in conversation with a nurse. This was my chance. Without a second's hesitation I walked out of the curtained cubicle and quietly, nonchalantly strolled down the hallway toward the exit door away from my captor. Passing right by the doctors and nurses, I felt like I was invisible and nothing could stop me. When I reached the automatic glass doors, they silently slid open, welcoming me to the free world. As I stepped through and the doors slid closed behind me, I paused to assess my situation. The street was 50 yards away and very busy. I could just run out into traffic, stop a car, get in and disappear forever. I turned my head back to look through the glass doors and saw that the federal agent was still talking to the nurse, totally oblivious to my absence. A snicker escaped my mouth. "Piece of cake," I said out loud.

However, when I stepped forward to execute my plan, I suddenly felt paralyzed. A cloud of confusion quickly enveloped me. What seemed so easy and so clear just seconds ago was now scrambling in my brain. I kept trying to propel my body forward, but it wouldn't obey. That's when I turned my head to the side and saw the nurse at the front desk looking at me. I'd finally been noticed. As she gazed at me intently, I slowly turned and headed back through the sliding glass doors. Then in a controlled pace, I started walking down the hall directly toward the agent.

"What am I doing?" I thought, panic-stricken, but it was as if I could not stop myself. Voices in my head now began screaming violently at me to turn back around, but something stronger wouldn't let me. Finally, I was standing directly behind my captor, yet neither he nor the nurse seemed aware of my presence. "You can still escape!" the voices said. "Turn around – it's not too late!"

But, instead of fleeing, I reached out my hand and touched the agent on the shoulder. Now I was committed. Startled, he turned around. When he saw me, he instantly paled. I saw pure fear in his eyes as a thousand questions of where I came from invaded his mind. As he stared at me in a speechless panic, I could tell he knew something almost went terribly wrong. Finally, I broke the icy moment.

"You ready to go?" I said. "Yeah, yeah," he stuttered. Still visibly shaken, he fumbled with his handcuffs before gratefully putting them on me. As I heard the familiar ratchet sound of the cuffs closing and felt the metal tightening around my wrists, my only thought was, "What the hell have I done!?!"

I spent the next week in a foul-smelling booking cell, every inch covered with grime. It was freezing. The metal benches and cement were ice cold to the touch. Since I was coming down off the dope, my bones ached. I wanted a smoke so bad I could have snapped somebody's neck for one. During this time, I went back and forth to a fancy federal courtroom where I was charged and arraigned. When I stood in front of the judge, filthy, and with chemical burns on my hands and still in my stocking feet, he refused my bail saying, "We all know what side of the law you're on Miss Caple." My feeling was right. They had me and they intended to keep me. I was returned to the putrid-smelling booking cell, then dressed in my jail issue khakis and taken back to inmate population.

That night as I lay in my cell alone, thoughts would not stop bombarding my mind. Why didn't I escape when I had the chance? What in the world stopped me? I wrestled with those questions for hours until I felt like exploding! Finally, pushed to the brink, I started screaming for the thoughts in my mind to shut up. Then miraculously, my mind got quiet and I heard one word -"Pray." Strangely, just the thought of it brought me comfort. But why? Praying was something I'd never done a lot of before.

Don't get me wrong; during my life, I experienced various run-ins with God. At age 14, I was "born again" on a beach in Hawaii, though I didn't really know what that meant. At 26, my well-meaning cousin dragged me to church where, despite being high, God baptized me with His Holy Spirit. The man there who prayed for me said God told him I was a drug dealer. I acted like I didn't know what he was talking about. Then at age 29, after doing dope every single day for years, I took a "vacation" to Idaho where my aunt and uncle ran a church. There I met Jesus. It was great, but a few months later, the vacation was over. I was back cooking dope.

Now at 35, I was in the bind of my life and the word "pray" was the only thing that made it seem better. Lying in my bunk, I pondered this strange situation. I was locked up with no hope for bail and a list of federal charges. I was stuck with my hands, literally tied, and there was nothing I could do but pray. So I did. And to my surprise it just poured out of me. Decades of anger, pain and hard-heartedness welled up in me, overflowing like a tidal wave. I couldn't believe I was confiding so deeply in someone I didn't know – God. I felt better than I had in years! What I didn't realize was that God had been waiting for this moment all my life. With incredible love and patience, He bore through my years of sin, eager for this moment when He would cause me to love Him as deeply as He loved me. I lay there praying for hours. It seemed like I couldn't stop and felt like I didn't want to. My journey had begun.

1. Recall the events leading up to your arrest (bondage). Try to recognize when and where God was present in these events.

2. Have you had a relationship with God before this time? Explain.

3. How do you feel about being in captivity?

CHAPTER TWO

"For everything that was written in the past was written to teach us, so that through endurance and the encouragement of the Scriptures we might have hope."
Romans 15:4

The above verse from the New Testament tell us that the Old Testament was written down for us so we can apply its lessons directly to our own lives today. *"The Captivity Series: The Key to Your Expected End"* is a study of the exiles in ancient Israel taken from the Old Testament Scriptures. Its purpose is to teach you about ancient Israel's imprisonment, then help you apply this knowledge to your own incarceration.

There are 39 books in the Old Testament. About two dozen of them speak in detail of the captivities of ancient Israel. This makes the subject of their imprisonment one of the most prevailing themes in the entire Bible. To date, there are over two million people in prisons in just the United States alone. Many of them, whether they know it or not, are God's elect for whom He has a **unique purpose.** This is why God filled the Old Testament with such a massive resource of information on Israel's captivities. Their story is to be used as a guidebook to lead today's prisoners to their created purpose through the vehicle of their exile.

From the beginning of my imprisonment, God gave me a hunger to read the Bible. I started from page one of Genesis and read to the very end of Revelation. Then I repeated the process over and over. Each time I went through the Bible, the Holy Spirit would teach me more about Israel's story. The more I learned, the more I realized that, although their imprisonment happened thousands of years ago, **their experience was exactly like ours today.**

When I applied the Scriptures to my captivity, amazing things happened: Changes took place in me. I developed a deep relationship with God. I started training in captivity for His purposes in my life. I even experienced the miraculous over and over again right in the middle of my incarceration. It was so incredible I wanted to share my newfound treasure with prisoners everywhere!

I took a poll once in a Bible Study I was teaching while in prison. I asked how many people read the entire Old Testament. Only one person raised her hand. Amazingly, the rest of the class, when questioned, didn't even know the Israelites went to prison at all!

Because of people's obvious lack of knowledge on the history of Israel's captivities, I am going to start this study with an overview of their journey in, through and out of exile. For some of you this will be the most difficult part of the study. Not everyone is a history buff. However, you need to know Israel's history in order to avoid opening yourself up to error in your interpretation of the text when the Holy Spirit speaks to you. One of the reasons I experienced so much success during and after my incarceration is because I became thoroughly versed in Israel's historical account. This enabled me to properly interpret the revelations God was giving me concerning my captivity. As you read on, don't forget to make notes when you feel the Holy Spirit may be speaking to you.

The History of Israel

The forefather of the Jewish race, Abram (later renamed Abraham by God), was born around 2166 B.C. God made a promise to Abraham that one day his descendants would take possession of a land called Canaan. Now modern day Israel, Canaan, was made up of some of the most fertile and lush lands in the world. This is why it was known as the *"land flowing with milk and honey."* (Exodus 3:8)

When Abraham was over a hundred years old, God began to fulfill His promise by giving him a son named Isaac. Isaac grew up and had a son named Jacob who then had 12 sons. Each one of them would become the forefather of the 12 tribes of Israel, making up the whole Hebrew nation.

One of Jacob's sons, Joseph, was the first prisoner ever mentioned in the Bible. Betrayed by his 11 brothers, Joseph was sold to slave traders who took him to Egypt, where he eventually ended up spending 13 years in an Egyptian dungeon. While in prison, God gave Joseph favor with the warden who put Joseph in charge of the entire prison. As the years went by, Joseph's administrative skills were developed to perfection, preparing him for the true purpose God intended for his imprisonment. Joseph would one day be used to save the world from famine!

When time for the famine approached, God warned Pharaoh, King of Egypt, through a dream. Unfortunately, neither he nor his magicians understood the warning. Then one of Pharaoh's officials recalled that, while he was in prison, Joseph had accurately interpreted his dream. Upon hearing this, Pharaoh immediately called for Joseph to be brought up from the dungeon. After listening to Pharaoh's dream, Joseph told him Egypt was soon to experience seven years of plenty followed by seven years of deadly famine. When Pharaoh and his officials heard this, they were at a loss as to how to save Egypt. However, Joseph had an answer. Using the administrative talents, he learned while in prison, Joseph advised Pharaoh to store up five percent of all of Egypt's crops during the first seven years of plenty. Doing so would insure Egypt would have enough food when the years of famine arrived. Seeing Joseph's wisdom, Pharaoh released

Joseph from prison, put him in charge of storing the grain and made him second in command over all of Egypt!

By the time the famine began seven years later, Joseph had stockpiled enough grain to sustain the lives of everyone in Egypt as well as all the surrounding countries. That's when his brothers, who were facing starvation, traveled to Egypt to buy grain. They came face to face with Joseph for the first time in years. Though difficult at first, they were finally reconciled. Then Joseph moved his entire family to Egypt so they could survive through the famine.

Years passed and a new Pharaoh came into power. Joseph was now gone and long forgotten. This king put the 12 tribes under his whip, forcing them to provide the labor, including the making of bricks for Egypt's massive building projects. The enslaved Hebrews began to cry out for God to deliver them from Egypt; but, for the next 400 years, they could only dream of the land God promised them through Abraham.

Four centuries later, the Lord God answered their cry and raised up a man named Moses. Through him, God performed miraculous signs and wonders against Egypt. Ten plagues were released on the city. Pharaoh was forced to let the slaves go. The Israelites were finally delivered from Egypt's powerful grip. The people started their journey to their long-awaited inheritance.

What began as an 11-day trip to Canaan turned into a 40-year long ordeal. While traveling through the desert, the Israelites rebelled against Moses and God. Then, when the people reached Canaan's border and were instructed to go in to take possession of the land, they refused out of fear! Finally, God's wrath overflowed, and He repaid the people's disobedience by making them wander in the desert until the generation that left Egypt died.

Forty years later, the next generation of children were grown up and ready to collect their inheritance. As the young nation prepared to cross over into Canaan, they were given a warning. They must continue to obey God's commandments in order to keep possession of the Promised Land. If Israel chose to obey God while in Canaan, He would supernaturally bless them in every way. However, if they rebelled, He would bring curses against them like famine, disease and pestilence. If after being repeatedly warned, Israel still chose to disobey God, He would deliver His final curse: **The Curse of Captivity.** Invaders would come and remove the people from their inheritance, taking them prisoners into distant lands.

Forewarned, Israel entered into Canaan around 1400 B.C. Through warfare, they took possession of the land from its inhabitants. Finally, the Israelites were in their Promised Land, which seemed to literally flow with milk and honey. But there was a danger lurking under the surface. Though the Israelites conquered the land, they didn't totally destroy all the native people as God had directed. Over the next generations, those survivors would intermingle with Israel then lead them into idolatry. This was a direct violation of God's commandments.

One of the first prominent people in the Bible to practice idolatry was King Solomon. He was known as Israel's wisest king, its richest ruler and the man who built the sacred temple in Jerusalem. Solomon was also the first Israelite king to be swayed into idol worship. He intermarried with many foreign women from the nations the Lord had commanded to be driven out of Canaan, who led Solomon into severe idolatry. The result of his sin was that the nation of Israel would split into two separate kingdoms. Ten tribes made up the Northern kingdom, and two, Judah and Benjamin, made up the Southern kingdom. Eventually, both kingdoms would end up in captivity.

The Northern Tribes immediately got off to a bad start when their new ruler, King Jeroboam, led them directly into idolatry. Afraid his people would defect back to Jerusalem because the temple was there, Jeroboam set up two golden calves on altars so everyone could stay home to worship. This was a direct violation of God's commandments. The northern kingdom began its steady downward spiral into exile.

As the generations passed, no reform took place; rather, each new king led the people deeper into idolatry, and God's feared curses became reality. Disease and famine ravaged the North, but the people did not heed the curses. The backsliding continued. Finally, after 200 years of continuous rebellion, God slammed down the curse of captivity upon the people like a hammer. In 722 B.C., God prompted the nation of Assyria to come and take the Northern kingdom captive and those 10 tribes fell into the hands of the brutal Assyrians. They were deported as prisoners to the Assyrian Empire, and none of them ever returned home. The Israelites suffered their first exile.

Meanwhile, the Southern kingdom, whose capital city was Jerusalem, fared slightly better, and lasted a little longer than the North. However, over the generations, they too took on all the perverse practices of the pagan nations around them. Once in a while, kings like Hezekiah and Josiah came into power, cleansing the land of its sin. But, for all the good they did, kings like Manasseh did 10 times more evil. During the 55 years he was in power, Manasseh built altars to other gods, bowed down and worshiped the starry hosts (astrology), practiced sorcery, witchcraft, divination and even sacrificed his own son to fire in the worship of the god Molech. When the people and the high officials of Judah began to follow Manasseh's lead, God's cup of wrath overflowed. God sent word through His prophets that, like Northern Israel, the Southern kingdom would soon go into captivity as well.

Around a half a century later, the Lord fulfilled His threat. He brought the curse of captivity upon the Southern tribes. He rose up Nebuchadnezzar, king of Babylon, to attack His disobedient people. First, Nebuchadnezzar took all the silver and gold vessels from Solomon's temple. Then, in 586 B.C., his armies laid siege on Jerusalem.

For two years, famine swept the trapped city, with the situation becoming so severe that the Israelites ate their own children in order to survive.

Finally, Nebuchadnezzar broke into Jerusalem, sacked it and burned everything to the ground. The people of Judah were then put in chains and forced to walk almost 1,000 miles to Babylon. There, they were placed as prisoners, in ghettos within the massive walls of the city. The second exile had taken place.

The Israelites were now praying for God to deliver them like He did so long ago in Egypt. However, this was not going to happen, or at least not right away. God's plan was to use Israel's captivity to bring about their repentance and to get them prepared for the purposes He planned for their lives. To begin this process, the Lord sent a letter into Babylonia containing instructions for the prisoners to follow while they were in captivity. Over the years, as the exiles obeyed those instructions, amazing things happened. They began to change, be repentant and prosper right in the middle of their imprisonment! By the end of their 70-year sentence, Israel's hearts were totally turned back to God. They were ready to pursue His purposes for their lives.

When it was time for the Israelites to go home, the Lord raised up a king named Cyrus to deliver them from their captivity. Leading the Median and Persian empires, King Cyrus attacked Babylon, and this, once mighty nation fell in one night. After the victory, Cyrus issued a decree for the Israelites to go home and rebuild Jerusalem. Finally, the exiles were free. The trial of their imprisonment was over! Now, they faced the new challenge of rebuilding their lives.

Three different waves of exiles returned to Jerusalem from Babylon. Each group had their own unique purposes and problems. Armed with a mission to rebuild Solomon's temple, the first wave of returnees hit Jerusalem in 538 B.C. Led by Zerubbabel, this group of exiles entered the burnt-out city and immediately went to work. Although they started off with a lot of zeal, their efforts were soon bogged down as opposition to their project arose from every corner. First, enemy attacks, then worldly distractions, came in to soften the Israelites' resolve to finish building. Finally, the attacks were so intense the people became discouraged. They discontinued their work on the temple, turning instead to concentrate their efforts on rebuilding their own homes.

For the next 18 years, the ex-prisoners abandoned the mission God sent them on and paid a high price because of it. Where at first the people prospered immensely, they were now struggling to make it. No matter how much seed the Israelites planted in their fields, they still harvested very little. Though they worked hard at their labors, they mysteriously possessed no wages to show for it. What went wrong? God had called for a drought on all the work of their hands. He sent word through the prophet Haggai that He was preventing Israel's prosperity because they abandoned the work on

His temple. When the people heard Haggai's message, they quickly returned to the mission. Because they were obedient to complete their assignment, their prosperity was returned.

The second wave of returnees entered Jerusalem in 458 B.C. This group was led by a man named Ezra, whose mission was to teach the exiles in Jerusalem the Word of God. Unfortunately, when Ezra got home, he discovered the people there were involved in a dangerous situation. They'd taken wives from amongst the women of other nations who practiced idolatry. This was a repeat of the same situation that led the Israelites into captivity in the first place. Thankfully, Ezra recognized the danger. He immediately commanded for all those marriages to be dissolved. When Ezra called for the Israelites to obey, they listened. The men sent away their foreign wives and children, preventing the curse of captivity from coming on them again.

Finally, in 432 B.C., a man named Nehemiah led the third wave of returnees back to Jerusalem. While still in the land of captivity he heard that Jerusalem's walls were broken down, leaving the city unprotected. After getting permission from the Persian king to travel to Jerusalem to repair them, Nehemiah went home and gathered the returned exiles together to begin the work.

Like the first wave of exiles, Nehemiah's group was also attacked while they attempted to rebuild. However, no matter what threats were launched against the exiles, they did not stop building. In fact, so fierce was Nehemiah's resolve to finish the job, his people held a weapon in one hand, ready to fight, while continuing to work on the wall with the other. Because Nehemiah refused to let anything stop the Israelites from completing their mission, the wall was finished in a miraculous 52 days!

After all the years of struggle, Jerusalem was finally intact. The glorious temple and the protective city wall were restored, and the people were living an abundant life, actively involved in the service of their God. Israel reclaimed their land of milk and honey! Over the years, the exiles learned an important lesson. As long as they kept their eyes on God and the purposes He gave them, they could overcome all obstacles, prosper and NEVER return to captivity again.

Israel's story is one of victory - not over their captivity - but victory through it. God used their time of imprisonment to give them back their Promised Land. He wants to do the same thing for you. Believe it or not, you also possess an inheritance flowing with milk and honey. Through this study, you are going to discover how God wants you to take hold of it through the vehicle of your captivity. So, let's begin applying the experiences of ancient Israel's exiles to your incarceration so you too can obtain your Expected End!

Lesson Two

1. *"For everything that was written in the past was written to teach us, so that through endurance and the encouragement of the Scriptures we might have hope"* (Romans 15:4). According to this verse, the Old Testament was written down so you can learn from it and apply it to your own experience. What parts of Israel's story stand out to you the most and why?

2. Do you see a direct connection between you and the ancient Israelite captives?

3. What parts of their story give you hope and why?

CHAPTER THREE

*"Then the Lord will scatter you **[take you into captivity]** among all nations... Among those nations you will find no repose, no resting place for the sole of your foot. There the Lord will give you an anxious mind, eyes weary with longing, and a despairing heart. You will live in constant suspense, filled with dread both night and day, never sure of your life. In the morning you will say, 'If only it were evening!' and in the evening, 'If only it were morning!' - because of the terror that will fill your hearts and the sights that your eyes will see."*
Deuteronomy 28:64-67 (*Author's interpretation - from the list of blessings and curses*)

How did you end up in prison? Some think that is easy to answer – you broke the law, you were arrested, then you went to jail. However, where does God fit in with it all? Parallel examples of what you are experiencing in your imprisonment are found throughout Scripture. The verses above are from the list of blessings and curses in the book of Deuteronomy. This particular Scripture I call the "curse of captivity." If it seems to perfectly describe what you are going through since being incarcerated, do not be surprised. The ancient Israelites experienced the same thing when they were imprisoned thousands of years ago.

The "curse of captivity" was originally given to the Israelites prior to their entering into the Promised Land of Canaan. It was a prophetic word warning the people that, if they didn't continue to obey God's commandments while living in their new inheritance, God would remove them from the land by the hand of invaders who would take them into captivity. Unfortunately, the Israelites did not heed the warning. They were taken into exile, first in 722 B.C., at the hand of Assyria, then again in 586 B.C., by the Babylonians.

For me, the discovery in the Bible of the captivity curse settled many disputes as to who was responsible for our imprisonment. Many say the devil did it, while others insist that it was our own fault. However, most agree that a loving God would never bring us into a horrible place like prison. Well, Scripture says differently. It **is** God Who brings you into captivity, but only as a result of your sin. I remember the moment I read the Scripture above from Deuteronomy and got this revelation. It changed my life because it meant God planned my imprisonment, so He would do something wonderful with it! (Romans 8:28)

Why would God take you into captivity? Number one, because you sinned against Him and broke fellowship with Him. The Bible says, *"Long ago, even before He made the world, God chose us to be His very own..."* (Ephesians 1:4 TLB).

God picked you to be His own before He even called the world into being! Now, that is heavy! It should give you a better idea of why God hated your life of sin on the streets. Your actions created separation from Him. To heal this relationship, God takes you into captivity, cleansing you of your sin and restoring you back to Himself.

The second reason why God will take you captive is because He has a purpose for your life other than the one you were pursuing. The Bible says, *"Everything got started in Him and **finds its purpose in Him**"* (Colossians 1:16 MSG).

God didn't create you so you could live a life of your own choosing. He made you for His purposes, ones that can only be found in Him. God is your Creator. He alone knows what you were created to be. The second chapter of Ephesians says, *"For we are God's workmanship, created in Christ Jesus to do good works, which God prepared in advance for us to do"* (Ephesians 2:10).

Before you were born, God made a special plan for your life. Unfortunately, on the streets you were chasing after your own plan, not His. Everyone was created by God to serve a unique purpose, but most have no idea what this purpose is. In fact, untold numbers of people go through life pursuing things they think they are supposed to do without ever consulting God to find out what He actually made them to be. This is the main reason God brings you into captivity: **To transform you into whom you were originally created to be, to reveal and give you His special purpose.** The Bible has a name for this purpose - it is called your **Expected End.**

*"For I know the thoughts that I think toward you, saith the Lord, thoughts of peace, and not of evil, **to give you an Expected End**"* (Jeremiah 29:11 KJV).

Everyone has an Expected End, but few ever find it. You are going to learn through this study that your captivity is specifically designed by God to prepare you for your assignment and help you discover what it is. The above verse, about your Expected End, comes from a chapter in Jeremiah titled *"A Letter to the Exiles."* This letter was originally sent to the ancient Israelite captives imprisoned in Babylon. In it, God promised a certain future for each one of them. Amazingly, He intended to use their imprisonment to bring this future to pass. The same promise is for you who are in prison today. It may be hard for you to believe this right now, but God is going to use your captivity for your benefit and His glory by fulfilling your wildest dreams!

So, how could something like the "curse of captivity" fit in with all this glorious-sounding stuff? God gave the list of blessings and curses to the Israelites to help keep them on the right track while they lived in Canaan. Using the blessings as incentives, He promised to supernaturally increase those who would continue to obey His commandments. However, catastrophes in the form of curses would come upon those who chose to disobey. Let's take a closer look at the blessings and curses so we can fully understand the purposes God intended for them. First, the list of blessings:

"If you fully obey the LORD your God and carefully follow all his commands I give you today, the LORD your God will set you high above all the nations on earth. All these blessings will come upon you and accompany you if you obey the LORD your God:" (Deuteronomy 28:1-2).

"The Lord will grant that the enemies who rise up against you will be defeated before you..." (v. 7).

"The Lord will send a blessing on your barns and on everything you put your hand to..." (v. 8).

"The Lord will open the heavens, the storehouse of His bounty, to send rain on your land in season and to bless all the work of your hands..." (v. 12).

"The Lord will make you the head, not the tail. If you pay attention to the commands of the Lord your God that I give you this day and carefully follow them, you will always be at the top, never at the bottom" (v. 13).

God offered His people incentives to do good by promising He would bless the lives of those who chose to be obedient to him. Notice how the verses in Deuteronomy are worded.

"The Lord will grant," "The Lord will open," "The Lord will make."

These Scriptures make it obvious Who is in control of the universe. God is God and His power can accomplish anything. In the above Scriptures, the Lord promised to direct people, circumstances, even nature itself, to make sure His obedient people got blessed. But what would happen to those who choose not to obey? God says they would be cursed.

"However, if you do not obey the Lord your God and do not carefully follow all his commands and decrees I am giving you today, all these curses will come upon you and overtake you:" (v. 15).

"The Lord will strike you with wasting disease..." (v. 22).

"The Lord will turn the rain of your country into dust and powder..." (v. 24).

"The Lord will cause you to be defeated before your enemies..." (v. 25).

"The Lord will afflict you with...confusion of the mind... You will be unsuccessful in everything you do..." (vs. 28-29).

When we are in disobedience to God, we are in sin. Sin separates us from God and His purposes for our lives. Disobedience also brings consequences. In Deuteronomy, God said those consequences would come in the form of curses and He would be the enforcer. Notice again, how the wording of the Scripture proves God's sovereignty and ability to carry out His threats. *"The Lord will strike," "The Lord will cause," "The Lord will afflict."*

The Lord is willing and able to move the very forces of nature in order to bless His obedient children. However, He is also ready to stop the rain from falling, cause total defeat and make His people unsuccessful in everything they do. Why would God do what appears to be such horrible things to His own people? **Because of His love for us, He works to deter us from continuing in our sin, which keeps us from entering into our inheritance, and His presence.**

Unfortunately, even after the ancient Israelites were told about the curses, they still chose to rebel against God. Because they did, He brought catastrophe upon them. The Israelites suffered through famine, pestilence and drought, yet continued in their disobedience until it was too late. But, too late for what? The ultimate curse God said He would enforce on them was the "curse of captivity."

"Then **the Lord shall scatter you** [take you into captivity] *among all nations..."* (v. 64).

The "curse of captivity" was the final blow. The other curses before it were designed to bring on pressure to persuade the Israelites to stop sinning against God. Unfortunately, the people didn't listen to the warnings, so God brought this final curse upon them. He sent invaders to take the Israelites into captivity.

When I first read the list of curses in Deuteronomy, I realized that, while I was on the streets, God was striking me with each one of them. Over the years, acquiring chemicals to cook dope became more difficult. It involved a lot more risk. Finally, because of all the federal restrictions, I resorted to robbing stores to get the supplies I needed. Meanwhile, it seemed like I was always battling with someone who ripped me off, teed me off or tipped me off to the cops. I suffered increasing *"drought, famine and pestilence,"* and it was just as the Scripture warned. I became unsuccessful in everything I put my hand to. Back then I just thought I was cursed, but now I know I truly was! God brought all this apparent misfortune against me to dissuade me from continuing in what I was doing. Unfortunately, instead of letting the pressure of the curses stop me, I pressed forward into my sin with even more resolve until finally God brought the curse of captivity crashing down on me.

Thinking back on your life on the streets, can you remember one thing after another going wrong? Maybe you lost your kids, your house, your car, or all your deals started going sour. Whatever it was you probably got to the point where you felt like your life was "cursed." Imagine that! All those apparent "bad luck" circumstances were not just random coincidences; they were the curses of God. Like the Israelites, you did not pay attention to those red flags until it was too late. Then you were so sick in your sin God prescribed the only remedy possible – captivity. Now, He has your attention, doesn't He? Well, this was the plan all along.

Like the rest of the curses, the "curse of captivity," with all its trouble, is designed to drive you into the arms of the Lord. The weighty pressure of your captivity experience is meant to create in you a desperate need to seek God for help, and relief from your situation. Let's read the whole curse again.

"Then the LORD will scatter you [take you into captivity] *among all nations... Among those nations you will find no repose, no resting place for the sole of your foot. There the LORD will give you an anxious mind, eyes weary with longing, and a despairing heart. You will live in constant suspense, filled with dread both night and day, never sure of your life. In the morning you will say, 'If only it were evening!' and in the evening, 'If only it were morning!' --because of the terror that will fill your hearts and the sights that your eyes will see"* (vs. 64-67).

"An anxious mind and a despairing heart!" What a perfect description of the mental and emotional trauma we go through when we are first incarcerated. In the beginning of my captivity, I lived in *"constant suspense,"* never knowing what would happen next. As the feds investigated our case, more and more evidence popped up, tightening the noose further around my throat. Finally, one of our co-defendants agreed to testify against the rest of us, which sealed our doom. We battled in the federal court for two long years before we finally lost. I was sentenced to 151 months in Federal Prison. During all of this, my mental, physical and emotional harassment was so great, I was overwhelmed.

Now I know God allowed all of those awful circumstances to bring about His ultimate purpose: To drive me back toward Him, in a desperate need for His help. During this time, I began to seek the Lord with all my might. The "curse of captivity" was performing its intended function, prompting me to run into the waiting Arms of my Savior. And run I did – full speed ahead without stopping!

You've been cursed with captivity, but only so the pressure of the curse can be used to bring you to God and all the wonderful purposes He has in store for you! So now what? The first thing to do is break the curse. The Bible says the only way to do this is to accept God's Son, Jesus Christ, as your Lord and Savior.

"Christ redeemed us from the curse of the law by becoming a curse for us, for it is written: 'Cursed is everyone who is hung on a tree.' He redeemed us in order that the blessing given to Abraham might come to the Gentiles through Christ Jesus, so that by faith we might receive the promise of the Spirit" (Galatians 3:13-14).

When Jesus hung on the Cross - He took all the curses heaped on you, including the "curse of captivity," and put them on Him. Then, because He was resurrected from death, He defeated those curses, bringing freedom to those who accept Him. By this same sacrifice, Jesus also won for you the right to receive the blessings of Abraham. Take a minute. Reread the list of blessings in Deuteronomy 28 and know they can be yours, once you ask Jesus into your life.

So, does this mean, if you accept Jesus as Lord, the "curse of captivity" will be removed and you will go home tomorrow? Probably not. The curse will be broken, but God brought you here for a reason: to change you, to have a personal relationship with you and to prepare you to go in and possess the Expected End He planned for you. However, you must start with Jesus! If you haven't accepted Him as Lord and Savior of your life, do so now, and the curse will be broken. Please pray this prayer with me.

"Lord God, I acknowledge that I have sinned against You. I have disobeyed Your commandments. I am asking You for Your forgiveness. I realize now that I am under the 'curse of captivity.' I also acknowledge Christ died on the Cross, becoming a curse for me. He was raised to life to redeem me from that curse. He makes me eligible for all Your covenant blessings. I ask Jesus, right now, to come into my heart so I can begin my journey toward You and the marvelous inheritance You have prepared for me. In Jesus' Precious Name, I pray. Amen."

Lesson Three

1. The Bible says, *"Everything got started in Him and finds its purpose in Him"* (Colossians 1:16 MSG). On the streets, do you think you were following after God's purposes or your own?

2. What were the purposes you were chasing? What were you trying to achieve?

3. The Bible says, *"For I know the thoughts that I think toward you, saith the Lord, thoughts of peace, and not of evil,* **to give you an Expected End"** (Jeremiah 29:11 KJV). Do you believe God has a better purpose for your life than the one you were pursuing?

4. The Bible says, *"However, if you do not obey the Lord your God and do not carefully follow all his commands and decrees I am giving you today, all these curses will come upon you and overtake you:...* Then **the Lord shall scatter you [take you into captivity]** *among all nations..."* (Deuteronomy 28:15, 64). What actions caused you to be put under the curse of captivity?

5. Read this verse and then answer the following. *"Christ redeemed us from the curse of the law by becoming a curse for us, for it is written: 'Cursed is everyone who is hung on a tree.' He redeemed us in order that the blessing given to Abraham might come to the Gentiles through Christ Jesus, so that by faith we might receive the promise of the Spirit"* (Galatians 3:13-14). According to this verse, what did Christ do for you on the cross?

CHAPTER FOUR

Nothing Can Substitute For Your Expected End!

"In the ninth year of Hoshea, the king of Assyria captured Samaria and deported the Israelites to Assyria... All this took place because the Israelites had sinned against the LORD their God ... They worshiped other gods and followed the practices of the nations the LORD had driven out before them..."
2 Kings 17:6-8

In 1406 B.C., the Israelites left the desert to enter Canaan. Less than seven centuries later, in 722 B.C., they suffered their first exile into the land of Assyria. The Bible says their captivity *"took place because the Israelites had sinned against the Lord their God."* The next verse goes on to say what sins were responsible for Israel's exile.

"They worshiped other gods and followed the practices of the nations the Lord had driven out before them."

In this chapter, we are going to study the two sins that sent Israel into exile. These are the basis of why you were also put under the "curse of captivity." Let's start with the first half of the Scripture, which talks about how Israel *"worshiped other gods."* In the book of Deuteronomy, God issued this direct warning to His people:

*"After you have had children and grandchildren and have lived in the land a long time - **if you then become corrupt and make any kind of idol,** doing evil in the eyes of the LORD your God and provoking Him to anger... **The LORD will scatter you** [take you into captivity] among the peoples..."* (Deuteronomy 4:25, 27).

God's message was clear. If the Israelites began practicing idol worship after they moved into their new inheritance, He would take them into captivity. However, even though Israel was warned, they still didn't listen. Slowly after entering the Promised Land, the people began to worship other gods in the form of idols. Exactly what is an idol? Thousands of years ago, idols were statues made of gold, silver, wood, or stone. The ancient Israelites believed these lifeless, man-made objects possessed real power to control their prosperity, fertility and even the weather for their crops. This may sound silly, but whether you realize it or not, when you were on the streets, you fell under the same deception.

Idols are not just a thing of the past. They exist today, taking on all kinds of forms like money, drugs, alcohol and even people. Webster's dictionary defines the word *idol* as "any object of ardent or excessive devotion." So, according to this definition, an idol doesn't need to be a statue made of gold, but anything we make the center focus of our life. However, only God has the right to be in this position because He is the One who gave us life. Unfortunately, prior to coming into prison, we were giving our attention to everything but God. So, in essence, we were practicing idol worship. The Bible says we were taken into captivity because of it.

The reason you were chasing after idols is because you thought they would bring you some kind of happiness. People are constantly looking for ways to feel better. They are desperately trying to find some kind of satisfaction to fill up the emptiness inside of them, often turning to drugs, alcohol or even food. But what causes someone to be so unhappy in the first place? According to the Bible, two things; **they don't have God or their God created purpose.** The Bible says,

*"He has made everything beautiful in its time. He also has planted eternity in men's hearts and minds **[a divinely implanted sense of a purpose working through the ages which nothing under the sun but God alone can satisfy]**..."* (Ecclesiastes 3:11 AMP).

Nothing under the sun can bring you complete satisfaction except for God and your Expected End! On the streets, you tried to make yourself feel better with drugs, sex, or whatever idols you were pursuing. Unfortunately, those things didn't fill your empty feeling. In fact, it only hurt more as your search took you further away from the Creator and your true, created purpose.

I remember that when I was on the streets, I always felt something was missing. No matter how high I got or how much money I possessed, the feeling never went away. In fact, the more things I tried, the worse I got. Finally, I remember getting to the point where I was so miserable, I just wanted to die. However, I wasn't the type that would kill myself; so, I picked fights with the biggest, meanest people in the drug world in an attempt to provoke someone into doing it for me. Many tried but, fortunately, none succeeded.

In contrast, when I was released from prison, things were totally different. I was now, in a relationship with God. Through my captivity, He gave me my Expected End. Possessing my own unique purpose meant that the empty void once controlling me was gone. And thus, so was my pattern of searching for fulfillment through idols. In fact, my God-given purpose empowered me so much, I didn't need to fight the urge to do drugs because I no longer desired them! My life was filled with God and my created purpose, **so I was completely satisfied.**

Unfortunately, other ex-cons I knew didn't do as well. Lots of them, even the Christians, went back to doing dope and crimes. Eventually, they were sent back to prison. Why? Well, even though some of them built a relationship with God while they were inside, none took possession of their Expected End during their captivity. Remember, Scripture says only two things can bring total satisfaction to someone's life: God and purpose. The Christians who returned to prison didn't have the second half of the equation; hence they were still anxiously searching for satisfaction in idols.

It is not enough to get God while you are in prison; you must also get the future He has for you. My husband Robert, who did 17 years, is a good example of this. When he was on the streets, he pursued the idols of money and drugs. Then he got arrested, came to the Lord and spent his time inside studying the Bible. By the time Robert was released, he was in an abiding relationship with the Lord. He also possessed vast Scriptural knowledge. Unfortunately, once he was on the outside, he discovered he needed more than this to make it.

When Robert was released, he didn't know what his God-given purpose was **which meant he possessed only half of the equation!** The result was that he went right back to the same old behavior pattern he followed before his arrest. He started searching for something to bring him the satisfaction he lacked. He struggled with cigarettes and alcohol. He even commented more than once that he would return to drugs if he weren't on probation. Robert also struggled with handling stress. Though he was a faithful, hard-working employee, he was miserable wherever he worked. This caused him to jump from job to job, in search of that special something he knew was missing. However, every time he started a new job, it didn't take long for the initial relief to wear off, and his same old miserable feelings would creep in again.

By the time I married Robert, his pattern of searching for satisfaction was in full bloom. Because of the frustration he felt, he came up with a new idea every week for us to try out. I remember one day he called me and said we should drop everything to enroll in barber school so we could start a business cutting hair in people's homes! Don't misunderstand me, I am not trying to down being a barber, but I already knew what my Expected End was, and this was not it! I also knew that the dozens of other ideas my husband was coming up with were just his attempts to substitute for something he didn't even realize he was missing: God's true purpose for his life!

Robert, like so many other Christians, struggled through his existence because he didn't know what his Expected End was. I remember the day the Lord began to reveal to Robert his true, created purpose. It changed his life! No longer plagued with a weary toiling feeling, he stopped pursuing different idols. **The behavior pattern that put him into prison was gone!** It was removed by the power of his Expected End! Though he was a wonderful husband when I married him, he became the man of my dreams after his revelation.

Nothing can substitute for your Expected End! You need it and absolutely must have it, but you will never find it by following after idols. In fact, idols will only lead you away from your true purpose. The Bible says, when Israel followed after idols, their lives were ruined.

"They despised and rejected His statutes and His covenant which He made with their fathers and His warnings to them, and they followed vanity (false gods--falsehood,

emptiness, and futility) and [they themselves and their prayers] became false (empty and futile)..." (2 Kings 17:15 AMP).

Israel followed after the false idols of the world, and their lives became the very things the gods they worshiped were: false, empty and futile. The Bible calls idols false because they deceive you into believing you can find happiness in them. They are called empty because following them won't bring you the fulfillment your true God-given purpose will. They are called futile because following them is a waste of your time. **You will never find your Expected End in your pursuit of idols!** In fact, idol worship will just get you to where you are totally out of control! On the outside, I did things that, if it weren't for God, would be considered unforgivable. I was no different than the ancient Israelites who became so desperate in their idol worship they even sacrificed their own children in the fire to the god Molech. (Leviticus 20:3)

You might be thinking you would never do this. However, in our own way, each one of us, including me, sacrificed our loved ones and ourselves to the flames, in order to try to get our fill. How many times did you drop your kids off with family or even a stranger so you could pick up a sack of dope? Perhaps you left them somewhere because you were too high to care about them? Do you see that your desperate search to find satisfaction was overriding your concern for anyone else? **This is why you must take possession of your Expected End while you are in captivity, because it alone will prevent you from returning to idols.** This study is going to show you how to find out what your purpose is!

Now, let's return to the first Scripture listed in this chapter. We are going to study the other sin that put Israel and you into captivity.

"They worshiped other gods and followed the practices of the nations the Lord had driven out before them."

The two sins above are directly related. The worship of other gods is what the people of the other nations in Canaan practiced. The above Scripture from 2 Kings says Israel sinned by following the examples of those people. Have you ever heard the phrase "monkey see, monkey do?" Well, that is what happened to Israel. They saw the people of the other nations practicing idol worship, and began to do what those people were doing.

When the Israelites first crossed over into Canaan, they fought its inhabitants in order to take possession of the land. Prior to this warfare, the Lord issued specific instructions to His people on how they were to deal with their Canaanite captives. His instructions were:

"When the LORD your God brings you into the land you are entering to possess and drives out before you many nations—the Hittites, Girgashites, Amorites, Canaanites,

*Perizzites, Hivites and Jebusites, seven nations larger and stronger than you—and when the LORD your God has delivered them over to you and you have defeated them, then **you must destroy them totally. Make no treaty with them, and show them no mercy. Do not intermarry with them... for they will turn your sons away from following me to serve other gods...*"* (Deuteronomy 7:1-4).

The conquest for Canaan was almost a total success. Israel won the battles, but failed to obey God's instructions concerning the people of the land. Instead of totally destroying the Canaanites, the Israelites left some of them alive. Israel even made treaties and intermarried with those people. Eventually, a deadly consequence arose from those alliances. The Canaanites spiritually poisoned the Israelites by teaching them how to practice idolatry. The Bible says the people of Israel ended up in captivity because *"**They imitated the nations around them** although the LORD had ordered them, '**Do not do as they do,**' and they did the things the LORD had forbidden them to do"* (2 Kings 17:15).

The Israelites mimicked the behaviors of the people of the world and ended up in prison for it. This is exactly what happened to you on the streets! You allowed people into your life that influenced your behavior. The more you were around them, the more you did as the Scripture said, *and "imitated"* them. You got high, wrote bad checks, robbed people, you name it. And you ended up in captivity for it!

None of us are exempt from this. Every drug I ever did I learned how to do from one of my "friends." I smoked pot, snorted coke and shot dope because somebody I was around was doing it. I learned how to deal by watching other dealers. I learned how to cook from other cooks. I allowed people in my life to turn my heart toward the idols of this world.

At first, I didn't want to admit that people could influence me so much. I've always been a leader, not a follower. However, I learned you should never underestimate the power that people of this world can have over your life. In Deuteronomy, where God commanded Israel to totally destroy the Canaanites, He said the people of this world were "larger and stronger" than Israel, meaning their influence was bigger than His people could resist. No matter what kind of person you may be, no one is exempt from worldly influences. This is why God commands us to totally remove those people from our lives.

Let's look at Solomon, the wisest king to lead Israel. He spoke 3,000 Proverbs, wrote 1,000 songs and could describe any kind of plant, animal, bird or reptile. The Bible says, *"God gave Solomon wisdom and very great insight, and a breadth of understanding as measureless as the sand on the seashore."* (1 Kings 4:29). But even though Solomon was a brilliant and powerful king, he was still swayed into severe idolatry by the people he allowed around him.

"King Solomon, however, loved many foreign women... They were from nations about which the LORD had told the Israelites, 'You must not intermarry with them, because they will surely turn your hearts after their gods' ...his wives led him astray. ...his wives turned his heart after other gods, and his heart was not fully devoted to the LORD his God..." (1 Kings 11:1-4).

Solomon's foreign wives led him to sin against God by following after idols. Because of Solomon's sin, the nation of Israel broke up into two idolatrous kingdoms, both ending up in captivity.

You are called by God to minister to the people of the world, not to "intermarry" with them. If you do, it is inevitable you will incorporate some of their behaviors as your own. One of the biggest reasons you are in captivity now is because of the associations you made while you were on the streets. Now that you know that the Bible says you will be taken into exile for those kinds of relationships, you need to be very careful not to get involved with them again.

Many times while I was still on the inside, I saw a believer's walk shipwrecked by the people they were hanging with. Time after time, I watched a person fall because they got caught up in the mix. They would stop going to church and Bible studies. Then they would start taking part in all kinds of drama: gossiping, fighting, stealing, even drugs and homosexuality. Jesus said,

"And if your right hand causes you to sin, cut it off and throw it away. It is better for you to lose one part of your body than for your whole body to go into hell" (Matthew 5:30).

This may sound pretty extreme, but what it means is that you need to go to extremes to cut yourself off from people who will steer you in the wrong direction. Right now as you're reading this, the Holy Spirit may be convicting you of a relationship or friendship you are currently in that is detrimental to your walk with God. If this is the case, do not test God.

Obey Him immediately! Discontinue the association. This may seem harsh, but if you had done this on the streets, you might not be here now.

Intermingling with the people of other nations was a trap that snared Israel over and over again. In fact, even though they knew this particular sin was one of the reasons they went into captivity in the first place, they still intermarried with the people of foreign nations after they got out! However, they are not the only ones who repeated this sin. Did you know the number of people who return to prison after being released is astronomically high? The reason many of them end up coming back is because they choose again to get involved in the same activities the people of the world are involved in.

If you are planning on hanging out with your old crowd when you are released, you might as well ask for your bunk to be reserved because you will be back. The Bible says so. Israel's associations with the people of the world led them into captivity. Your associations did likewise. Whether you are in or out, don't repeat the same mistakes again.

Lesson Four

1. The Bible says, *"He has made everything beautiful in its time. He also has planted eternity in men's hearts and minds [a divinely implanted sense of a purpose working through the ages which nothing under the sun but God alone can satisfy]"* (Ecclesiastes 3:11). According to this Scripture, what are the only two things in this world that can bring you total satisfaction?

2. The Bible says that one of the reasons Israel went into captivity was because *"they worshiped other gods...."* (2 Kings 17:8). What idols were you pursuing on the streets in an effort to find satisfaction?

3. The Bible says the other reason Israel was taken into captivity was because *"they... followed the practices of the other nations the Lord had driven out before them"* (2 Kings 17:8). Who were you hanging out with on the streets? How did those people influence your behavior?

4. Do you understand that the idols you were pursuing and the people you allowed to negatively influence your life contributed to your being put under the curse of captivity? Will you think twice before getting involved with idols or the wrong people again?

CHAPTER FIVE

FORCED SUBMISSION

"Then the Philistines seize him, gouged out his eyes and took him down to Gaza. Binding him with bronze shackles they set him to grinding in the prison. But the hair on his head began to grow again after it had been shaved."
Judges 16:21-22

My face was smashed against the cement floor because the correctional officers were pinning me down and cuffing my hands behind my back. I was being taken to lockdown **again,** for fighting **again!** Three of them escorted me from the yard to the front of the facility, then threw me into a holding cell. As soon as the cell door opened, the pungent odor of urine hit me in the face. The smell was strangely mixed with a hint of citrus from the orange peels that laid with the half-eaten sandwiches on the floor, which were leftovers from the sack lunches given to new arrests.

As the door slammed behind me, the face of the captain we called the "redheaded stepchild" loomed in the door window. "So you're down here again!" he barked, causing steam from his hot breath to fill the glass. "You know as long as you don't fix your @x!?@! attitude, we will keep throwing you in the hole!"

He was right, but I still didn't plan on doing any changing. He barked something else then disappeared, leaving only the sound of his combat boots echoing down the hallway. Since I was his most regular "customer," I knew he would be on a mission to make my stay as unpleasant as possible.

As I looked around for a place to sit without vomit on it, I knew making it unpleasant wouldn't be hard to do. I was not in a regular lockdown situation. I would be held in booking for my entire disciplinary time. This facility didn't have separate segregation housing for females, so when one of us got in trouble, we were taken on an all-expense-paid trip to booking.

But it wasn't exactly what I would call a vacation. The noise was constant: 24/7 with people screaming and crying, begging for phone calls, meds or a shower. Some would bang endlessly on the metal doors, while others would yell at them to shut up. I got up and went to the cell window just in time to see a drunken woman run past, stumbling down the hall while resisting the cops. Quickly, the "redheaded stepchild" and one of his evil twins jumped her, the twin stomping on her feet until she was subdued. Now whimpering, she was dragged across the floor by one arm into a cell, the door slammed behind her.

This is how it went in booking. As I turned to walk away from the window, a guy in the cell across the hall signaled me. I stopped and he flashed me, hoping I would do the same in return. Disappointing him, I turned away. "Not interested," I thought. I had more pressing problems. Like how long was I going to stay here this time and when were they going to bring me a mattress and a blanket. It didn't matter that both would be filthy. I was cold and tired.

For me, this was the hardest part, the freezing cold air pouring in from the overhead vent. Everything my body touched was frigid: ice cold metal bench, freezing cold cement floor. I grabbed the roll of toilet paper and started throwing gobs of wet tissue at the vent in an attempt to block off some of the air, wondering all the while if there was enough paper to do this and wipe the toilet so I could use it.

I admit that I was tired of making my regular visits to lockdown. It was starting to wear me out. It would be totally different if they put me in some cushy segregation cell like the men got. They were housed in a room with a bed and blankets, reading and writing materials and, of course, a shower. Now, that I could get used to! Then it wouldn't matter how many times I got into trouble because it would be like going to my very own hotel room! But there was to be no stay in the Hilton for me. Every time I acted up, off to booking I would go!

I'd been a fighter my whole life. I was an arrogant, aggressive, loud mouthpiece of dirt that always ran the show. I never let anybody tell me what to do. I thought I was all that, and then some. Now, I was locked up and surrounded by a bunch of cops who thought they could do as they pleased. My response to them was "I don't think so," which only got me thrown in the hole. On the other hand, I wondered why God wasn't sticking up for me. After all, I was reading His Bible. In fact, I was reading it all the time! Didn't this mean He was supposed to get me out of these kinds of situations?

I walked over to the window, avoiding eye contact with my new "friend" across the hall, and peered out the glass in hopes a trustee would go by and pass me a cigarette. "When did I start that fight?" I wondered, my mind retracing the time. "Hmm, it must have been about one o'clock," I recalled with disappointment. This meant the trustees wouldn't be down in booking for hours and I needed a cigarette now!

Spinning around with a kick, I sent a now stiff bologna sandwich skidding across the floor. The last time I asked someone to sneak me smokes, I ended up in a WWF wrestling match to try to keep possession of them. The captain and the lieutenant tag-teamed together against me, myself, and I. At the thought of that event, I giggled, but the memory gave me only brief joy. Quickly, I came back to the reality of having to go through this again. How many days or weeks would it last this time?

Thinking on it, I turned back around, leaning against the cold iron door. I looked out again into the now vacant hall. Where was a cop when you needed one? I knew it would take forever to get a stinking mattress. It always did. The more I thought about it, the more irritated I got.

Just then, I could hear the door to medical being opened. They were bringing in the "rat" I got into a fight with. She was screaming something about her rib being broken and her girlfriend, who was in the fight also, was right behind her. She kept hysterically yelling her lesbian lover's name over and over. The rat was my co-defendant. I just found out she was going to testify against us in Federal Court. Suddenly, I felt sick, not only at the thought of this, but also because I hadn't eaten all day and could feel my diabetes kicking in.

Plopping down on the sticky floor, I quickly resigned myself to the fact I wouldn't be getting food any time soon. So, instead of worrying about it, I sat there dwelling on my co-defendant's betrayal. Soon my hateful thoughts started to well up in me until they overflowed. Leaning over, I put my mouth up to the crack of the door and began chanting, "Bring me a mattress and blanket" over and over, but with no results. Finally, I stood up and turned around to mule kick the door. BOOM! BOOM! BOOM! The noise echoing in the hallway sounded like mortar fire. "One of you useless @#! !@x! cops bring me a @#@! x! @ blanket NOW!!", I screamed. Then, far off at the end of the hall, I heard their laughter. They were, on purpose going to let me freeze just to teach me a lesson.

Hours passed as I listened to those two women screaming and crying. As for the cops, whenever they went by my window they would taunt me and I, of course, always said something not so neighborly back. Finally, tired of that game, I figured if I went to sleep, I could sleep my lockdown time away. So, I lay down on the 10" wide metal bench trying to balance there as the cold invaded me to the bone. When I awoke from my restless nap, I ached. My clothes and hair stunk like the foul water in the toilet.

Yeah, for sure I was tired of it. I would have given anything to be back in my bunk smoking a cigarette. How many times was I going to put myself through this before I got it right? As I continued to think on it, my stress rose. I could feel my blood sugar plummeting. Sure enough, minutes later, I went into a seizure.

I don't know how long after, I awoke to find myself sitting upright with a cup of sugared Kool-Aid in my hand. I heard the nurse say, as she was being escorted from my cell, my blood sugar level was 69, dangerously low. That's when I noticed a sack lunch sitting by me.

"It's about time!" I spat in disgust at the C.O. who was with her. My outburst only prompted him to slam the door as he left.

Man, was I tired. I was totally worn out. I was fighting everyone: cops, inmates, the courts, and though I didn't realize it, God himself. I felt weak, like I couldn't take it anymore. Slowly, I slumped down against the cold cement wall. I finally reached the breaking point, which was exactly what God was waiting for.

At once, I was aware that He was right there, because I felt shame. His presence brought the conviction that all my actions were way out of line. As I sat there feeling His hand of chastisement, I clearly heard Him say that He wanted me to stop fighting and surrender to my captivity. The thought of it made my flesh squirm. Surrender was not in my vocabulary. My pride could never allow me to do so.

Shaken, I took another drink of the Kool-Aid, then pulled a bag of Fritos out of the sack lunch. As I munched on the chips, my blood sugar began to rise and my mind got clearer. How could God possibly expect me to do what He was saying? As I pondered on this, I also stopped to take a real good look at my surroundings. My little cell was cold and disgusting. Down the hallway, I could still hear my adversaries battling with the guards. It seemed nothing changed, but suddenly everything was very different. A light went on. I understood what was really happening. All this time I refused to yield, so God, through my circumstances, was playing "uncle" with me, twisting my arm until I would say, "I give.".

Revelation flooded in. Instantly I knew God had appointed this nasty booking cell just for me. In fact, everything I was going through was being used by Him to bring me into submission: the cops, and even the girl who would testify against me, were all acting in accordance with God's sovereign plan. The awakening was so impressive that I was actually left with a desire to behave, and cease from my rebellion.

Right then, I heard footsteps coming down the hall. Now, feeling totally energized, I jumped up and raced to the window in time to see the back of a C.O. as he passed by. Here was my first chance to obey God. Trying to sound as sweet as possible, I called out to the officer,

"Hey, hey excuse me.", I said. But he ignored me and kept going. Irritated, but still trying to be polite, I continued.

"Hey C.O., do you think I could get a Bible?"

This made him stop. Slowly, he turned around with a surprised looking smirk on his face and said, with a lot of emphasis,

"No, you can't have any books in there."

"That's all right," I replied, holding back the slur of obscenities rising in my throat. "God will bring me one."

At this, he spun around laughing and swaggered away. As I watched him go, I clenched my fists in frustration, trying not to explode. I could tell this surrender thing was going to be very difficult. So, still feeling more than slightly peeved, I prayed out loud,

"Show him, Lord, get me a Bible!"

The next day they actually took me out for a shower. They even gave me clean khakis to put on. After I finished, I went to throw my stinking uniform into the clothing barrel and noticed it was empty. This was unusual because it was always overflowing with dirty uniforms. As I stepped up to dump in my clothes, I looked down and, lo and behold, at the bottom of the barrel was a Bible! A sign? A miracle? God answered my prayer! As I reached down to claim my precious prize, I firmly decided to do whatever God told me, no matter what.

I still failed and took more trips to booking after this. However, the difference was I spent my time there praying and singing to God instead of wrestling with the cops. Meanwhile, as the months went by, the problems I had with my attitudes and behaviors began to disappear. Good characteristics took their place. I also began experiencing a realization that my entire captivity was in some strange way being used by God for my benefit. Though I couldn't see how at the moment, God would definitely show me over time. Little did I know then that I was on my way to experiencing things I would never dream could happen to me.

Lesson Five

1. Recall the times in your incarceration when you broke the rules.

2. Did you have to face any consequences spiritually, physically, or otherwise?

3. Now, can you see God's hand in those difficult times? In what ways?

CHAPTER SIX

"...any nation or kingdom that will not serve this same Nebuchadnezzar king of Babylon and put its neck under the yoke of the king of Babylon, that nation will I punish, says the Lord, with the sword, with famine, and with pestilence, until I have consumed it by [Nebuchadnezzar's] hand ...Bring your necks under the yoke of the king of Babylon... and live."
Jeremiah 27:8, 12 AMP

It was 586 B.C., Jerusalem was being attacked by hordes of Babylonian forces pounding away at its defensive walls. In the middle of the attack God sent word to His people. Surrender to the Babylonians and live. Resist the enemy and be punished by Him through their hand. Unfortunately for Judah (the Southern kingdom), they chose to resist and, as God warned, paid severely for it.

The Babylonian armies staged a two-year-long attack, during which time those trapped in the city were consumed with famine and pestilence. Facing starvation, many resorted to cannibalism. Those who survived were later killed or taken captive when the Babylonians broke through the walls. As for the city itself, Jerusalem's grand houses and the sacred temple were sacked and burned to the ground. The Israelites lost everything because they refused to surrender to their enemy as God had instructed them.

In the beginning of my incarceration, I was much like Jerusalem, under siege and refusing to wave the white flag. Because of my resistance I too was *"destroyed"* by God, repeatedly punished at the hand of my captors until I was broken. Once I stopped fighting, and bowed my neck under my jailers' yoke, as the Scripture above says, I began to *"live"* and experience victory in my captivity. Let me tell you something very important. It is human nature to resist attack, but it is God's nature to use attack to break down our resistance.

Why would God command His own people to surrender to a vicious invading army? Because Israel's impending captivity was **His** doing. He ordered it. God raised up the Babylonian nation to come attack His city and imprison His people. Let's look at the proof of this in the book of Habakkuk.

"Look at the nations and watch—and be utterly amazed. For I am going to do something in your days that you would not believe, even if you were told. I am raising up the Babylonians, that ruthless and impetuous people who sweep across the whole earth to seize dwelling places not their own. They are a feared and dreaded people; they are a law unto themselves and promote their own honor... They fly like a vulture swooping to

devour; they all come bent on violence. Their hordes advance like a desert wind and **gather prisoners like sand"** (Habakkuk 1:5-9).

The Babylonians were the instrument God chose to carry out the curse of captivity on Judah. As hard as this was for the Israelites to believe, it shouldn't have surprised anyone, since it was not the first time God used a pagan nation against His disobedient people. Over one hundred years earlier, in 722 B.C., the Northern kingdom, after centuries of idolatry, was taken into exile at the hand of Assyria. In the book of Isaiah, God said this about His use of Assyria against the North:

"Assyria is the whip of my anger; his military strength is my weapon upon this godless nation...But the king of Assyria will not know that it is I who sent him. He will merely think he is attacking my people as part of his plan to conquer the world" (Isaiah 10:6-7 TLB).

Unknown to Assyria they, like Babylonia, were operating under God's sovereign control when they took the Israelites into exile. History proves throughout the ages that God used whatever agencies He desired to carry out the curse of captivity on His people. But how does this relate to you and your incarceration? Scripture says, *"I the Lord do not change..."* (Malachi 3:6). Which means you can expect that what God did before, He will do again.

Would you believe God called the entire judicial system to arrest and imprison you? The Scripture in Habakkuk said you wouldn't believe it, even if you were told. Nevertheless, it is true. Today, God's chosen instruments to carry out his plan of captivity are the police, the feds, judges, courts, detention centers and prisons. Every person and part of the justice system is God's Babylonia and Assyria of today. Just as in ancient times, God is divinely directing their actions concerning your exile. Let me explain.

God uses the justice system to achieve His specific purposes. To find out what they are, let's take a look at what Habakkuk said concerning God's use of Babylonia as Israel's captors.

"...O Lord, You have appointed [the Chaldean] **to execute [Your] judgment,** and You, O Rock, have **established him for chastisement and correction"** (Habakkuk 1:12 AMP).

The Babylonians (also known as the Chaldean) were appointed by God to perform three jobs concerning the Israelite captives, *"judgment," "chastisement and correction."* Let's quickly look at each task.

First, the system of law is used to deliver *"judgment"* on lawbreakers. Sin has consequences. On the streets you broke the law, then were consequently arrested and imprisoned because of it. This process is called judgment. It is what God uses to stop you dead in your tracks and prevent you from continuing on the path you were on. You see, before you can begin your journey toward your true purpose, you must be taken off the streets. **So you can be separated from the things that lead you into sin.** God uses the process of judgment to achieve this. Though being imprisoned is painful, it is really the first step toward the wonderful purpose the Father has for you.

Secondly, the judicial system is appointed by God for *"chastisement."* To chastise means to discipline. One of the main functions of the judicial system is to restrain evil through punishment. When you enforce a law on someone, to some degree it will stop them from continuing in their lawless behavior for fear of the punishment they may receive. What happened to me in booking is a good example, but let me give you another one.

My co-defendants and I fought our case for almost two years. During this time we were transported to the Federal Courthouse for numerous hearings. Well, on those trips, I would wreak total havoc with the federal marshals. I would threaten and verbally harass them, refuse to go into the holding cells, kick and punch dents into the metal toilet stalls and throw stuff at the cameras. Once, I even stole the gun box keys in an attempt to escape.

Because of my actions, I was hassled big-time by the marshals. They would drag me down the hallways by my arms and legs, throw me up against the walls, shackle me, hand to foot, for hours **while inside** the holding cells. The marshals even went so far as to call the detention center I was in and told them to throw me in the hole when I got back from court! So, what is my point in telling you all this? I finally got so tired of being punished by them, I stopped acting up! The chastisement "Babylon" put on me achieved what God appointed it to do: brought an end to my sinful behavior.

Then, once I stopped rebelling, I took the third step in God's process by beginning to act in the right manner. This is why the Scripture says Babylonia is established for *"chastisement **and correction.*"** The two go hand-in-hand. Once sinful behavior is stopped, then and only then can correct behavior take its place and changes begin to happen in you.

Our present-day Babylonia is the tool God uses to change our attitudes. Did you know that repeatedly in the Old Testament God called Assyria and Babylonia by the names of tools? In Jeremiah 27:6 AMP, He calls Nebuchadnezzar King of Babylon *"my instrument."* In Jeremiah 50:6, Babylon itself is called *"the **hammer** of the whole earth."* In the book of Isaiah, Assyria is referred to as a *"rod,"* an *"ax,"* a *"saw"* and a *"club"* (Isaiah 10:15). God called these nations by the names of tools because He used them as such, to demolish old attitudes in His captive people, then rebuild in them new ones. I know this is true from the pounding I received from the Babylonian **"hammer."** Just as a metal smith will pound on raw materials to make them into a perfectly formed instrument, my hammering was good and necessary to achieve God's purposes in my life.

Thinking this is "good" may be hard for some of you to accept because, to the average convict, the judicial system is considered our enemy. We think the cops are corrupt, the judges are wrong and the laws are unfair. The consensus is the legal system can do whatever it wants to, and get away with it. Well, be assured the ancient Israelites felt the same about their jailers as we do. Just reread the description Habakkuk gave of the Babylonians.

"...the Babylonians, that ruthless and impetuous people... They are a law unto themselves..."

Sound familiar? This is exactly how we view the judicial system today. Nothing has changed for thousands of years, but our prejudiced attitude against them must change since it causes us only harm. We must push aside resentment, rebellion and suspicion while submitting to their authority, for it is God's will that we do so. Let's see what the book of Romans says about this.

"Let every person be loyally subject to the governing (civil) authorities. For there is no authority except from God [by His permission, His sanction], and those that exist do so by God's appointment" (Romans 13:1 AMP).

First, let's get it straight about what authorities you need to be submissive to. According to this Scripture, **all of them!** The Bible makes it clear; there is not one cop or judge who hasn't been placed in their position except by God, so you need to submit to them all. What happens when you don't?

"...he who resists and sets himself up against the authorities resists what God has appointed and arranged [in divine order]. And those who resist will bring down judgment upon themselves [receiving the penalty due them]" (Romans 13:2 AMP).

I know this Scripture is true from first-hand experience. When you resist the authorities, you are in reality, directly resisting God and will face consequences because of it. When Jerusalem was being attacked by the Babylonians, God told His people to surrender, but they refused. Because they did not obey, they faced severe judgment, losing everything including their freedom!

God's plan of submission is designed to bless you. This will be very hard for some of you to believe, especially when you need to submit to an official who seems totally unjust. However, the Bible promises if you obey that person God will bring **GOOD** to you through them. Look at proof from the next Scripture in Romans.

*"Let every person be loyally subject to the governing (civil) authorities. ...For **he is God's servant for your good**"* (Romans 13:1, 4 AMP).

You may argue as to how the C.O. who hassles you or the judge who gave you so much time could possibly be a servant for your good? Well, let me tell you. My judge gave me a 13-year sentence and thanks be to God, he did. All that time scared the heck out of me - prompting me to seek God in an intense way.

The result of my desperate search was that I met my Lord. Then He changed me, empowered me, and gave me the future and the ministry I have today! As far as my 13-year sentence goes, well, God removed it anyway! All the incredible things I possess now are a result of a judge who was being a servant for my good when he gave me a lot of time!

God works in everything for the good of those who love him (Romans 8:28). Look at my co-defendant who testified against me in trial. I wouldn't have been convicted if it weren't for her. That means I would have been released and gone back to my old ways, never experiencing the incredible life I live now!

As long as the governing authorities do not contradict God's laws, you are required to submit. So, next time you feel you are being wronged by an official or a situation, remember God will use it to bring you more blessings than you could ever imagine if you will just trust what He is doing and obey.

Lesson Six

1. Habakkuk 1 and Isaiah 10 explain that the nations of Assyria and Babylonia were both used by God to carry out the curse of captivity on the Israelites. Malachi 3:6 says, *"I the Lord do not change."* What do you think these Scriptures mean in reference to the judicial system, your arrest, and incarceration?

2. The Bible says, *"Let every person be loyally subject to the governing authorities. For there is no authority except from God [by His permission, his sanction] and those that exist do so by God's appointments."* (Romans 13:1 AMP). List some of the authorities you've dealt with since your arrest. Be specific. At present what is your view of these people?

3. According to the Scripture above, which of those people were ultimately appointed to their position by God?

4. According to the Bible, what happens when you don't obey them? Completely write out Romans 13:2.

5. The Bible says, *"Let every person be loyally subject to the governing authorities... **for he is God's servant for your good"*** (Romans 13:1, 4 AMP). When you obey the governing authorities, you are obeying God. Therefore, He will bring **good** to you through them. Write down an instance where you can now see good coming to you through an official, especially if it was in a difficult situation.

CHAPTER SEVEN

"My times are in your hands; deliver me from my enemies and from those who pursue me."
Psalm 31:15

I f you want to see a prisoner cringe, just mention the word "time", because, in essence, that is what imprisons us. Most people in captivity calculate time according to how many days, months or years are left until they hit the gate, if ever. When a prisoner thinks about how God might view time they get scared and confused. Scriptures such as a thousand years are like a day to God (Psalm 90:4) will cause us to think that God views a life sentence as a mere drop in the bucket. So, is there anything good about time unless it's short?

Our view of time needs to change. We need to learn about the redemptive quality of time, and then use it for our benefit instead of it using us. In this chapter, we are going to look at how God uses time to accomplish His purposes in our lives, and see the difference between man's time and the time of God's favor.

God does not live in time, but He created it and uses the passage of it to accomplish His will. Concerning the time you have to serve, God wants specific purposes worked out in you through the vehicle of your time. To find out what those purposes are, let's refer to the Old Testament book of 1 Kings.

The passage we are about to study is from a series of prayers King Solomon gave when he dedicated the newly completed temple in Jerusalem. During this ceremony, Solomon prayed for the Israelites who would eventually go into captivity in the generations to come. His prayer is important for you now because it will clue you in on the purposes God wants you to complete during your incarceration. Let's take a look at what Solomon prayed, then discover what his prayer means to you.

"When they sin against you - for there is no one who does not sin - and you become angry with them and give them over to the enemy, who takes them captive to his own land, far away or near; and if they have a change of heart in the land where they are held captive, and repent and plead with you in the land of their conquerors and say, 'We have sinned, we have done wrong, we have acted wickedly'; and if they turn back to you with all their heart and soul in the land of their enemies who took them captive, and pray to you... then from heaven, your dwelling place, hear their prayer and their plea, and uphold their cause" (1 Kings 8:46-49).

King Solomon prayed for the captives to do three things during their time of exile: *"have a change of heart in the land where they are held captive," "repent and plead with you in the land of their conquerors,"* and *"turn back to you with all their heart and soul in the land of their enemies."*

God wants you to change, repent, and turn fully back to Him while you are imprisoned. His desire is for you to be transformed into a new creation, recognize and repent of your old lifestyle, and turn completely to Him by surrendering to His will for your life; this means getting prepared for and possessing your Expected End. These are God's purposes for your time and He wants you to complete them while you are here. Notice in his prayer, Solomon repeatedly asked for these purposes to take place in the captives **while they were imprisoned.** Look at the prayer again.

*"If they have a change of heart **in the land where they are held captive**... repent and plead with you **in the land of their conquerors**... and if they turn back to you with all their heart and soul **in the land of their enemies...**"*

These Scriptures make it is obvious that God wants you to complete His purposes while you are still on the inside. Why? Because if you don't, you won't make it when you get out! Or you will just end up living a half-full existence for the rest of your life.

Since my release, I've lived such an incredibly abundant life. So much so, that if I didn't know better I would think I was charmed. Well, luck had nothing to do with it. The reason my life is so good now is because I completed God's purposes while I was still inside! During my time, I repented and turned away from my past. I was eternally changed. Plus, I took possession of my Expected End. All those things combined gave me the power to be victorious and claim my rightful inheritance once I was released. I am now living in my land flowing with milk and honey because I completed these purposes while still behind bars.

Now, let me give you a warning. Scripture says that if you don't fulfill God's purposes while you're inside, you could stay longer or come back after you're released. Look at what the prophet Jeremiah said concerning this.

*"**[Their chastisement will continue until it has accomplished its purpose]** for My people are stupid, says the Lord [replying to Jeremiah]; they do not know and understand Me. They are thickheaded children, and they have no understanding. They are wise to do evil, but to do good they have no knowledge [and know not how]"* (Jeremiah 4:22 AMP).

According to this verse, the chastisement of your captivity will continue until you complete God's purposes for your time! This is no joke! I've seen it happen to literally hundreds of inmates who got out, but eventually ended up coming back. You see, in some way, shape or form those people did not complete God's purposes while they were inside, so they didn't make it when they were released. In the upcoming chapters, I will be showing you exactly why completing these purposes can ensure that you never come back to captivity again.

What will God do for the prisoner who strives to complete His purposes? The question should be what wouldn't He do! God possesses unlimited power and ability to help you with any issue. In fact, no one has a clue as to the wonderful things God is ready to do for His people who are in captivity. However, there is a condition to God's hand moving on your behalf. Look again at Solomon's prayer. Notice the order in which he prays for the prisoners.

"...if they have a change of heart in the land where they are held captive ...and repent ...and if they turn back to you with all their heart and soul in the land of their enemies... **then...hear their prayer and their plea and uphold their cause."**

Solomon made it clear that *"if"* the captives strived to fulfill God's purposes during their time *"then"* God would hear their prayers and uphold their cause. God is ready and able to release His power on your behalf, but you must first commit yourself to doing His will. Don't think you need to be perfect in order to receive God's help. You just need to have a heart that seeks to obey God. It is a Scriptural fact that obedience on our part brings reward. So *"if"* you choose to pursue God's purposes, *"then"* you can expect to be blessed.

I love how Solomon, at the end of his prayer, asked God to hear the captives' cries and *"uphold their cause."* Can you guess what Israel's biggest cause was? Why the same thing as yours and mine, to go home! Did you know one of Webster's meanings to the word *cause* is "lawsuit?" Think about that! Many of you are praying for God to uphold your cause in court so you can go home. Well, according to this Scripture, God will answer your prayer if you are working toward fulfilling His purposes!

In the beginning of my time, I can remember fervently praying for God to bring us victory in our case, but every time we went to court, we lost! I realized later, after I knew more about the character of God, that He wasn't letting me go for a reason. Because I wasn't ready yet. I hadn't completed His purposes so I wouldn't have made it if I had gotten out! God doesn't want you to fail. He wants you to experience a lasting transformation so you can live abundantly for the rest of your life! Completing His purposes will ensure this.

Now very quickly, I want to talk about the difference between man's time and the time of God's favor. Which one did you get? Many inmates feel they were sentenced to man's time, which means they got more than they should have. If this is your case, you need to learn about the time of God's favor. Let's look at exactly what this is by first confirming who is in control of your time, God or man? The Bible says, *"My times are in Your hands; deliver me from my enemies and from those who pursue me"* (Psalm 31:15).

The Psalmist recognized this important truth: God is in control over all your time, including the amount of time you serve! He is sovereign and, as the above Scripture states, can deliver you from anything, including the time to which man sentenced you.

This deliverance from the enemy of time has a biblical name; it is called "the time of God's favor." Look at this Scripture from Isaiah.

"This is what the LORD says: **'*In the time of my favor*** *I will answer you, and in the day of salvation I will help you; I will keep you and will make you to be a covenant for the people, to restore the land and to reassign its desolate inheritances,* **to say to the captives, Come out, and to those in darkness, Be free!'"** (Isaiah 49:8-9).

The word "favor" can mean **to make an exception to the rules!** So, even though your paperwork may say you have 20 years, God's favor can make an exception by changing your sentence! However, under what conditions are you eligible to receive the time of God's favor? Under the condition you are striving to fulfill the purposes God ordained for your time. Remember what Solomon said, *"if"* you are pursuing God's purposes, *"then"* He will *"uphold your cause."*

In the following chapters, we are going to study in detail God's three purposes so you can begin to walk them out during your stay. When you start taking steps toward totally surrendering your life to God, you will see Him come to your rescue and show you things you could never imagine!

Lesson Seven

1. Solomon prayed the following prayer for the captives, "*When they sin against you- for there is no one who does not sin- and you become angry with them and give them over to the enemy, who takes them captive to his own land, far away or near; and if they have a change of heart in the land where they are held captive, and repent and plead with you in the land of their conquerors and say, 'We have sinned, we have done wrong, we have acted wickedly'; and if they turn back to you with all their heart and soul in the land of their enemies who took them captive and pray to you... then from heaven your dwelling place, hear their prayers and their plea, and uphold their cause*" (1 Kings 8:46-49). Solomon prayed that the captives would accomplish three purposes during their time. What are those purposes?

2. According to the above Scripture, where does God want these purposes completed?

3. The Bible says, "*My times are in Your hands; deliver me from my enemies and from those who pursue me*" (Psalm 31:15). According to this Scripture, who is in control of your time, including the time you have to serve?

4. The word "favor" can mean "to make an exception to the rules." God's favor can include making an exception to the amount of time you have to serve. God can show the time of His favor to those who are completing His purposes during their incarceration. Completely write out Isaiah 49:8-9. This is God's promise of favor to the captives.

"And if they...repent and plead with you in the land of their conquerors and say, 'We have sinned, we have done wrong, we have acted wickedly'; ...then from heaven, your dwelling place, hear their prayer and their plea, and uphold their cause."
1 Kings 8:47, 49

The First of God's Purposes for Your Time from Solomon's Prayer

Wouldn't it be nice if you could just say you were sorry for the crimes you committed then they would let you go home? You might laugh at this idea but there is more possibility to it than you realize. Saying you're "sorry" in a biblical way contains so much power it can literally affect your time.

The word for being biblically sorry is to be repentant. There are two things that really move God – sin and repentance. As far as your sin goes, God brought you here because of it. Let me say this again – your sin motivated God to move the entire judicial system, judges, cops and all, to get you here. Realizing this truth, can you now imagine how God will respond to your repentance? When you truly ask for forgiveness and turn from your sins, it will motivate Him to move mountains on your behalf!

There are millions of people in prisons across the world asking God to move their mountains, but many are getting no response. Why? They are asking for help without first repenting of their sins. The Bible says,

"Surely the arm of the LORD is not too short to save, nor His ear too dull to hear. But your iniquities have separated you from your God; your sins have hidden His face from you, so that He will not hear" (Isaiah 59:1-2).

According to this Scripture God does not hear the prayers of those who don't ask for forgiveness. This same biblical principle is what King Solomon said in his prayer. *"If they repent...* **then** *from heaven, your dwelling place, hear their prayer and their plea, and uphold their cause."* The Bible makes it clear, you must ask for forgiveness of your sins in order for your requests to be heard.

You would be surprised at the large number of people in prison who never admit to their crimes. My co-defendants and I were perfect examples. We spent years complaining about how the feds burned us. Even though we were totally guilty, we denied our charges because we wanted to get out. We lied to everyone about our guilt, including our families. I guess we even thought we could lie to God in hopes He would just overlook our sin and deliver us out of our captivity anyway. Unfortunately, what my co-defendants and I didn't understand is this: God is a righteous God who cannot overlook sin and **will not uphold the cause of those who don't repent of it.**

Right now a huge percentage of inmates are acting the same way my co-defendants and I did. They constantly complain about being burned by the courts. Or they claim they didn't do it and somebody else did. Some people lie about their case for so long they convince themselves they are not guilty. This disease of denial and unrepentance is out of control. It has reached an epidemic level in the prison population today.

Did you know the ancient Israelites acted the same way while they were in captivity? Totally ignoring their own sin, they steadfastly claimed their innocence and even blamed Assyria, Babylon and God Himself for their imprisonment. Because Israel refused to repent, the results were catastrophic. The people who went into exile in Assyria **never** came home. The captives in Babylon almost suffered the same result.

Though both groups pleaded with God to release them from their imprisonment, only the exiles in Babylonia made it back to the Promised Land. Why? They eventually fulfilled God's purposes for their time, including the purpose of repentance. I say eventually because it took the Israelites almost 70 years to repent of their past. Before that, they cried out to God to take them home, but He didn't respond.

Fortunately, a man named Daniel recognized Israel's sin of unrepentance and took it upon himself to plead with God in prayer on behalf of his fellow captives. In this chapter, we are going to study Daniel's power-packed prayer to see how it dramatically affected Israel's time and how it can affect your time as well. Daniel's prayer begins like this:

"In the first year of Darius son of Ahasuerus (a Mede by descent), who was made ruler over the Babylonian kingdom—in the first year of his reign, I, Daniel, understood from the Scriptures, according to the word of the LORD given to Jeremiah the prophet, that the desolation of Jerusalem would last seventy years" (Daniel 9:1-2).

Daniel starts his prayer by referring to the Scripture he read in Jeremiah 29, which said the Babylonian exile would last *"seventy years."* Verse 10 in chapter 29 of Jeremiah says,

"For thus says the Lord, When seventy years are completed for Babylon, I will visit you and keep My good promise to you, causing you to return to this place" (Jeremiah 29:10 AMP).

Here, the Lord promised to give the Babylonian captives the time of His favor. However, Daniel knew from Solomon's prayer that, for the captives to receive this promise, they must first be pursuing God's purposes. Since the seventy years were almost up and most of the captives hadn't repented, Daniel realized he must take immediate action. So he begins pleading with God in prayer.

*"I prayed to the LORD my God and **confessed**: 'O Lord, the great and awesome God, who keeps His covenant of love with all who love Him and obey His commands, **we have**

sinned and done wrong. We have been wicked and have rebelled; we have turned away from your commands and laws'" (Daniel 9:4-5).

The very first thing Daniel does in his prayer is fulfill God's purpose of repentance. He immediately starts off by confessing his sins and the sins of the exiles. The next thing he does is acknowledge the reason why he needed to repent.

*"LORD, you are righteous, **but this day we are covered with shame...** in all the countries where you have scattered us because of our unfaithfulness to you"* (Daniel 9:7).

Daniel started his prayer with repentance because the rest of the captives hadn't, which meant they were still covered with the shame of their sins they committed 70 years before!

This same shame is on thousands of prisoners today! Those who are still in denial of their crimes yet constantly complain about the unfair justice system and all the wrong done to them. As Daniel continues his prayer, he makes it clear that it was the people's own sins that got them placed in captivity.

"All Israel has transgressed your law and turned away, refusing to obey you. Therefore, the curses and sworn judgments written in the Law of Moses, the servant of God, have been poured out on us, because we have sinned against you" (Daniel 9:11).

Here, Daniel states that the curse of captivity was poured out on Israel because of their own sins, not anyone else's. The prisoners in Babylon, however, failed to acknowledge this. Unfortunately, they didn't understand how their un-repentance was greatly affecting their relationship with God and their ability to receive favor from Him. The next thing Daniel says confirms this.

*"Just as it is written in the Law of Moses, all this disaster has come upon us, **yet we have not sought the favor of the LORD our God by turning from our sins** and giving attention to Your truth"* (Daniel 9:13).

Israel was crying out to God for the time of His favor but hadn't received it because they weren't asking in the right manner, **through repenting of their sins.**

For the first two years I was down, I prayed a lot for favor concerning my time, but I didn't get it. Instead, I got sentenced to 13 years. However, after I read Daniel and King Solomon's prayers, I realized I was asking for favor in a way God would not respond to. Fortunately, once I stopped lying about my case and started confessing my sins, God then began to move on my prayer requests. He even upheld my cause in court by taking seven years off my sentence!

Daniel asked for favor in the right order. Only after, he confessed and repented did he then plead with God to fulfill His favorable promise to take Israel home. The next part of his prayer says,

*"O Lord, in keeping with all Your righteous acts, turn away Your anger and Your wrath from Jerusalem... hear the prayers and petitions of Your servant. For Your sake, O Lord, look with **favor** on Your desolate sanctuary... O Lord, hear and act! For Your sake, O my God, do not delay, because Your city and Your people bear Your Name"* (Daniel 9:16-17, 19).

Even though Daniel's plea was urgent because the 70 years were almost up, he still took the time to make his requests in the right order. Daniel confessed and asked for forgiveness **first** before daring to ask God to bring about the time of His favor. What was the result of his prayer?

*"**While** I was speaking and praying, **confessing my sin and the sin of my people Israel** and making my request to the LORD my God for His holy hill - **while** I was still in prayer, Gabriel, the man I had seen in the earlier vision, came to me in swift flight about the time of the evening sacrifice. He instructed me and said to me, 'Daniel, I have now come to give you insight and understanding. **As soon as you began to pray, an answer was given**...'"* (Daniel 9:20-23).

As soon as Daniel began to confess the sins of the captives, his prayer was answered! This proves how compelling repentance is to God! Notice Daniel mentions twice that *"while"* he was confessing, an answer was sent. I believe he made this point so you and I would really understand the power repentance has in getting our prayers answered!

Repentance changes our situation. Biblical scholars agree this powerful prayer of Daniel's was largely responsible for ushering in God's favorable time for Israel. Because of his prayer of repentance the "good promise" of a 70-year sentence (Jeremiah 29) came to pass. The first wave of returnees went home 70 years after the first captives arrived in Babylon.

I want to stop here to ask you a very important question. How far would you go to get out of serving your time? Would you continue to lie and work the loopholes of the legal system even if you were guilty? The Bible says if you confess your sins you will receive mercy. (Proverbs 28:13) Perhaps throughout this chapter the Holy Spirit spoke to you about coming clean with your crimes. Do not ignore His prompting. Do not fear doing what He is telling you to do. Though it will probably be one of the most difficult things you've ever done, **God guarantees He will uphold your cause if you will trust and obey Him.**

Finally, I want to quickly discuss the importance of asking for God's favor in the right manner because it is the manner in which Daniel approached God that made his prayer even more effective. Let's backtrack to Daniel 9:3:

"So I turned to the Lord God and pleaded with him in prayer and petition, in fasting, and in sackcloth and ashes."

Daniel didn't come to God with some casual minute-long prayer lacking in heartfelt sadness. The Scripture says he took off his robes and replaced them with coarse sackcloth to show his deep mourning over the sins of the captives. He also sat in ashes to symbolize the destruction brought upon the people by their sins. He literally pleaded with God while going through a period of fasting.

Daniel's actions show us the perfect example of the manner in which we should seek God during confession. The Amplified Bible's version of Daniel 9:13 gives us more insight on what our demeanor should be as we approach God in prayer.

"...Yet *we have not **earnestly begged for forgiveness** and **entreated the favor** of the Lord our God, that we might turn from our iniquities..."*

To be earnest means to "to be serious and intense" and "to act in a determined manner." To entreat means "to implore" or literally "to beg."

Have you seriously come before the Lord to confess? Are you determined to seek His forgiveness and be washed clean of your sins? I think we take the old "just ask for forgiveness" thing too lightly. Unfortunately, most of us were taught that all we need to do is mumble a few words in prayer in order to be forgiven, and then we can get what we want.

When I finally understood I needed to do much more than casually ask God for forgiveness, I felt very strange. My heart was still hardened from all those years of denial so I honestly didn't feel sorry for my sins. Thus, I thought if I came "begging" God for forgiveness I would be faking it and, of course, He would know. This is when the Holy Spirit showed me I just needed to be obedient to do as the Scriptures instructed.

So, I prayed Daniel's prayer. I did it in the same manner he did by fasting and petitioning God in a serious, determined way. As I took those steps of obedience, God took care of the rest. Slowly, over time, He began to show me the depths and ugliness of my sins. Then, sure enough, I began to be truly repentant. This is when my pleading became real, fueled by a deep, heartfelt intensity. Eventually, God even gave me the strength to take the next step of confessing my lies to my family and the authorities. Unfortunately, I took a long time to do this. I pray you do not make the same mistake.

Do yourself a favor – make Daniel's prayer your own. Read it, meditate on it and then pray it to God. Completely humble yourself like Daniel did. You will be amazed at how quickly God will respond! Daniel's prayer of confession and repentance changed Israel's entire future. It can change yours too!

Lesson Eight

1. The Bible says, *"Surely the arm of the LORD is not too short to save, nor His ear too dull to hear. But your iniquities have separated you from your God; your sins have hidden His face from you, so that He will not hear"* (Isaiah 59:1-2). According to this Scripture, what would keep God from hearing and answering your prayers?

2. This is the first purpose Solomon prayed for your time. *"If they... repent and plead with You in the land of their conquerors and say, 'We have sinned, we have done wickedly'; ...then from heaven, Your dwelling place, hear their prayer and their plea, and uphold their cause"* (1 Kings 8:47-49). According to this verse, what can you do to move God to hear your prayers and uphold your cause?

3. After the ancient Israelites spent almost 70 years in captivity without repenting of their crimes, Daniel interceded for them in prayer. In his prayer, Daniel gives the reason why the Israelites hadn't received the time of God's favor. *"Just as it is written in the Law of Moses, all this disaster has come upon us, **yet we have not sought the favor of the LORD our God by turning from our sins** and giving attention to Your truth"* (Daniel 9:13). According to Daniel, why hadn't Israel received God's favor?

4. Have you confessed your crimes (or sins) both to God and to man?

5. In what ways will your failure to confess affect your relationship with God? How will it affect God hearing your prayers? How will it affect your ability to receive mercy from God and get the time of His favor?

6. Spend some quiet time with the Lord. Go before Him seeking His forgiveness for your crimes. Ask Him for the grace to repent. Believe that once you do this, you will experience more of God, and His mighty hand will move on your behalf!

CHAPTER NINE

"...if they have a change of heart in the land where they are held captive... then from heaven, Your dwelling place, hear their prayer and their plea, and uphold their cause."
1 Kings 8:47, 49

The Second of God's Purposes for Your Time from Solomon's Prayer

Another purpose decreed for your time is that you change while you're here. God wants the old you, the one who always reacted to people and circumstances with anger, impatience, jealousy, immorality and selfishness to be transformed into a new person; one who will operate in the fruit of God's Spirit: love, joy, peace, patience, kindness, goodness, faithfulness, gentleness and self-control (Galatians 5:22-23). These are the characteristics God wants developed in you while you are here. In order for this to happen, however, you must have a change of heart. The Bible says,

"The heart is deceitful above all things, and it is exceedingly perverse and corrupt and severely, mortally sick! Who can know it [perceive, understand, be acquainted with his own heart and mind]?" (Jeremiah 17:9 AMP).

According to this Scripture, no one has a clue to the severity of the heart's sickness. In the Bible, the heart represents your mind, will and emotions. Therefore, what is in your heart controls your behavior. That means every decision you make, and every thought, word or action you take, springs out of a heart the Bible describes as perverse and corrupt. Is it any wonder we experience so much drama in our lives? Our deceitful hearts are directing everything we do!

Your heart must be changed in order for your behavior to change. Change is one of God's purposes for your time and, as Solomon's prayer indicates, it will affect whether or not God will hear, then answer, your requests while you are in captivity.

Your willingness to change will affect your ability to be successful for the rest of your life. God has an Expected End for you, one that will require godly character. However, the poisonous behavior in your heart right now can shipwreck your future. In order for you to be ready to take possession of your Promised Land, you must change. So exactly how do you begin? The Bible says,

"Our iniquities, our secret heart and its sins [which we would so like to conceal even from ourselves], You have set in the [revealing] light of Your countenance" (Psalm 90:8 AMP).

The only way you can heal your deceitful heart is by setting it in the revealing light of God's countenance, which is found in the pages of His Word. The Bible is a book filled with instructions on how to live life to the fullest, in a way that will please God. It also contains supernatural power to enable you to change. Hebrews 4:12 in the Amplified Bible says:

*"**For the Word that God speaks is alive and full of power** [making it active, operative, energizing, and effective]; it is sharper than any two-edged sword, penetrating to the dividing line of the breath of life (soul) and [the immortal] spirit, and of joints and marrow [of the deepest parts of our nature], **exposing and sifting and analyzing and judging the very thoughts and purposes of the heart.**"*

The way the Word works is by first exposing the wrong motives of your heart then applying its power to the deepest parts of your nature to change those motives. The result of this process is that you are transformed, step-by-step, into a new person, one filled with godly character. The Word possesses the power to do all this, but there is a catch. **You must actively put your attention to the Word in order for it to work.** This means you must **read** the Bible and then **do** what it says. Reading alone is not enough. You also must take what you learn and put it into practice. The Bible says,

*"Do not merely listen to the word, and so deceive yourselves. **Do what it says**"* (James 1:22).

In the beginning of my walk with God, I read the Bible all the time, but unfortunately I failed to take action on what I learned. The result was I remained unchanged! This is why I kept going back to lockdown all those times, because I was being a reader, not a doer. **You must actively give your attention to the Bible, reading it and doing it, for it to change you!**

Did you know a lot of the ancient Israelites who were in Babylon remained unchanged while they were there? After decades of being incarcerated, many of them retained the same bad attitudes and behaviors they possessed when they were first taken prisoner. Why didn't they change? Let me show you. Do you remember what Daniel said in his prayer?

*"Just as it is written in the Law of Moses, all this disaster has come upon us, **yet we have not sought the favor of the LORD** our God by turning from our sins and **giving attention to Your truth**"* (Daniel 9:13).

First, Daniel said Israel wasn't receiving God's favor because they failed to repent of their sins. But then, in the same Scripture, Daniel gave a second reason why the captives' prayers weren't answered. They hadn't been **"giving attention"** to God's **"truth."**

The Bible is God's truth. It is the only thing that can truly change a person's heart. What Daniel meant when he said the captives weren't *"giving attention"* to God's truth was they were not actively reading the Scriptures and living them out. This is why they were not changed!

Remember what Solomon said in his prayer: *"if"* the people had a change of heart while they were in the land of captivity *"then"* God would hear their prayers and uphold their cause. While I was in prison, I saw a lot of people refusing to change. Even the Christians (at times, I included) acted badly on a regular basis. My facility was like a big soap opera. There was always some kind of major drama going down. Everybody gossiped about everyone. There were always fights in the TV rooms over who got to watch their show. People would cut in line for the microwave or chow. There were jealousies at work and always one person in each room who made the rest of their cellmates miserable. There was even constant bickering amongst the people of the church and the choir. Why? People were refusing to change.

As sinful human beings, we are naturally selfish and prideful. This is why prison can be so difficult. There are hundreds of people trapped inside a barbed wire fence together, all fighting to get their own way. Is it any wonder we don't receive more answers in prayer? We must all learn to change.

However, change is absolutely the hardest thing for a human being to do. Our bad behaviors are so deeply rooted in us that it takes a lot for them to be removed. **For most of us, change is so hard that if we were not in a situation where we were forced to change, we never would.** This is where your captivity comes in. God uses it to **force** you into change. The Bible says, *"Before I was afflicted I went astray, but now I obey Your word"* (Psalm 119:67).

According to Webster's dictionary, *afflict* means, "to cast down, to strike, humble, trouble or injure." Before the Psalmist was afflicted, he was disobedient; but **when trouble came his way, he started to obey the Word of God.** What this proves is **affliction produces change.** The reality is that most people need to be afflicted before they will finally obey. This is why God uses your prison surroundings to force you into change. The affliction your captivity provides is designed to trouble you to the point where you will want to start obeying God's Word in order to find relief from your suffering. Let me show you how it works. The Bible says,

"In the same day [will the people of Judah be utterly stripped of belongings], the Lord will shave with the razor that is hired from the parts beyond the River [Euphrates]--even with the king of Assyria--[that razor will shave] the head and the hair of the legs, and it shall also consume the beard [leaving Judah with open shame and scorn]" (Isaiah 7:20 AMP).

In this Scripture, God said He would use Assyria to shave His captive people. He would make sure they were literally stripped of everything they owned. In the Old Testament, to be forcibly shaved was to be troubled, struck down and humiliated. These are the very definitions of the word affliction.

To force you to change, the Lord shaves you through the hands of His modern-day Assyria. He allows them to strip you of everything. Your family, your material possessions and, even more frustrating, the control you once had over your life.

Behind bars, you can't choose when you wake up, when you go to sleep, when or what you eat, or where you work. Daily, you stand in line to get your medication, food, laundry and even a shower. Now, you have no choice but to live in cramped quarters with others you may or may not like. Daily, you suffer affliction as you deal with all kinds of unpleasant people and situations. You must understand that God allows this because Assyria's shaving and stripping process produces change. **The many problems you face in captivity are being used by God to drive you to His Word so the power of the Word can transform you.**

So how are you handling your problem situations? Are you throwing a fit, being rude and insisting on your way? Or are you humbling yourself? Every second, of every day, your captivity will provide you with an opportunity to be patient or not, to forgive or not, to say you're sorry or not, or to gossip or not. In order to change you must, step by step, choose to respond in the right manner to each circumstance. The way this is done is by finding out what the Bible says to do in these situations, and then **DO IT.**

Does this mean you will have to put up with every undesirable thing while you're here? No, God will move on your behalf, but only after He is sure you are fulfilling His purpose of change. Remember what Solomon said: *"if"* you have a change of heart while you are in the land of exile, *"then"* God will answer your prayers.

In fact, God will do amazing things for people who fulfill His purpose of change! If you are consistently changing, the Bible calls you the *"uncompromisingly righteous."* Let's quickly look at some of the incredible blessings in the Bible for you!

"For you, Lord, will bless the [uncompromisingly] righteous [him who is upright and in right standing with You]; as with a shield You will surround him with goodwill (pleasure and favor)" (Psalm 5:12 AMP).

If you choose to change, God promises to *"surround"* you with *"goodwill, pleasure and favor."* Just a little favor from a lawyer, an official, your family, or even a total stranger can go a long way, so imagine what will happen when you are surrounded by it!!! You will get favor at work, favor in your room, favor in the courts and even the time of God's favor!

Another blessing accompanying change is an increased ability to hear from the Lord. When you are trying to walk out the Bible's instructions every day, God, in turn, will give you extraordinary supernatural guidance. Proverbs 3:32 in the Amplified says,

"For the perverse are an abomination [extremely disgusting and detestable] to the Lord; but His confidential communion and secret counsel are with the [uncompromisingly] righteous (those who are upright and in right standing with Him)."

God doesn't share His confidential communion with just anyone. According to Scripture, people who are walking upright receive His secret counsel. Think of the incredible benefits of being able to hear secrets from God! One word from Him can change your entire life! I know this from experience, for it was God who told me to appeal my case. When I did, I won! It was also God who told me my new release date six months before my victory in court!!! These are just some small examples of the miraculous things that happen to those who are willing to change!

While I was in prison, there were times when I would blow it by treating someone badly. Yet, God would still speak His wonderful mysteries to me. Why? Because, even though He knew I wasn't perfect, He also knew in my heart I really wanted to change.

The Bible says people who choose to change will receive the desires of their heart.

"The thing a wicked man fears shall come upon him, but the desire of the [uncompromisingly] righteous shall be granted" (Proverbs 10:24 AMP).

What desires do you have? God will grant them if you are walking out His purpose of change. Are your prayers being answered? If not, check your attitude. How are you doing in your pursuit of change? Ask yourself these questions. How do you react in your room when a conflict arises? In the TV room when you don't get to watch what you want? In the chow line or the microwave room when people cut in front of you? At the weight pile when there is a disagreement? In your unit when people are being loud or when others are talking "smack" about you? Examine how you are responding to each situation. Make an effort to be honest with yourself about your faults even if it makes you look wrong. Especially if it makes you look wrong! Then let the Word of God guide your behavior in each circumstance. As you walk out the Scriptures, you will see its power transform your life!

Just imagine what prison would be like if everyone were on a serious mission to be changed! Remember that the daily drama is just the shaving and stripping process God uses to expose your heart's attitude. Rejoice in every difficult situation you go through. Believe it or not, God allowed you to be afflicted to help you change so you could get ready for your future. So, be grateful you lost everything because now you can have it all!!!

Lesson Nine

1. According to Solomon's prayer in 1 Kings, *"...if they have a **change** of heart in the land where they are held captive...then from heaven, Your dwelling place, hear their prayer and their plea, and uphold their cause."* What is this Scripture asking you to do?

2. According to Scripture, the only thing that can truly change your heart is the Word of God. Completely write out Hebrews 4:12 in the space below.

3. The Bible says, *"Do not merely listen to the word, and so deceive yourselves. Do what it says"* (James 1:22). According to this Scripture, what two things must you do for the Word to take effect in you?

4. The psalmist says, *"Before I was afflicted I went astray, but now I obey Your word"* (Psalm 119:6). List all the different ways your captivity has afflicted you. How have those afflictions brought you closer to God?

5. List all the different behaviors and thought processes you know you need to change.

CHAPTER TEN

This God Thing Really Works

"Also, seek the peace and prosperity of the city to which I have carried you into exile. Pray to the LORD for it, because if it prospers, you too will prosper."
Jeremiah 29:7

Unbelievable, I was locked down again! This time I really blew it. I rushed a Correctional Officer. As I looked up toward the door I saw the face of the Major, who was the head of disciplinary, appear in the window of my cell. Then I heard the magnetic lock release and he stepped in with two other officers directly behind him. With a big heavy sigh, he put both hands on his hips and stared at me hard until it made me so uncomfortable I looked away. After what seemed like an eternity he said,

"Ms. Caple, you've repeatedly displayed this kind of behavior to such an extreme, we have no choice but to put you in a 90-day administrative segregation. During this time, you will stay here and be required to see a psychiatrist who will evaluate you every seven days. At the end of this three-month period, we will review your evaluations. If at this time we feel you are ready, we will return you to population. If not, your stay here will be continued."

When he ended his sobering announcement, he turned to leave; but as he reached the door he stopped and turned back around again.

"Frankly, Katie," he said, "I don't think you'll ever be fit to be placed in population again." With that and a final look of disgust, he shook his head and left.

"Ninety days?! Boy, I really did it this time," I thought to myself. I could definitely handle this amount of time in a regular lockdown cell, but 90 days in booking would be tough, even for me. As the reality of my predicament sunk in, I began to scold myself. How did I let this happen again? I was doing so well, actually changing into a different person; but one guard wouldn't stop messing with me, so I snapped.

Even though I screwed up again, one of the lieutenants, who recognized my transformation, allowed me to take my Bible to the hole. So, armed with God's Word, I sat wrapped in a wool blanket on a dirty plastic mattress thrown on the floor, scanning the pages for comfort.

Unfortunately, being in seg was not my only problem. I'd been down for over a year. I'd already gone to trial and lost. Now, I was waiting to be sentenced and was looking at up to 15 years in a Federal Prison. My co-defendants and I were fighting for a retrial. It just so happened that our motion was going before the court the next day.

Now, it was almost midnight. Knowing the direction of my life could drastically swing one way or another within a few hours made my tension unbearable. This was one of the reasons I spent the last three days in lockdown praying, singing and reading the Word. I was seeking some kind of supernatural help from God. The funny part of it was the cops. When they passed by my window, they would look in at me crazy-like. They weren't used to seeing me act this way. I was spending my time in the hole differently because, now, I was different.

Unfortunately, outside my cell, things were the same as always. Booking was packed with an assortment of people, like heroin junkies sick from withdrawals to regular folks with traffic warrants. All of them cold and dirty with no place to lie down for days, except the frigid cement. Tired of waiting, many were begging through the doors for the cops to process them out. As I sat there praying, I was doing a little begging myself.

"Lord, I need your help." I began, then, for a second, I heard a little voice questioning whether I was really talking to God or just myself.

"Tell me what is going to happen to me?" I continued, ignoring my previous thought. "Am I going to prison for the rest of my life or what?"

With this question, I closed my eyes to pause, then opened my Bible and looked down. The Lord led me to Jeremiah 29. As I read the title of the chapter *"A Letter to the Exiles,"* my heart leapt!

"Hey, I'm an exile." I thought, now sure God was going to give me a message. Quickly, I brought the Bible up closer toward my eyes to begin reading at verse 4.

"This is what the LORD Almighty, the God of Israel, says to all those I carried into exile from Jerusalem to Babylon: 'Build houses and settle down; plant gardens and eat what they produce...'"

"Whoa!" I said, my excitement immediately turning to panic. *"Build houses and settle down?!"* The very thought of what this might imply made me sick.

"Lord, does this mean I should make myself at home because I'm going to stay awhile?"

I paused to see if He would respond; but when nothing came but silence, I decided to continue looking for a different answer. Then I read further in verse 7,

"Also, seek the peace and prosperity of the city to which I have carried you into exile. Pray to the LORD for it, because if it prospers, you too will prosper."

What does this all mean? I wondered, as I stopped there for a second, but then quickly brushed it off to resume my hunt. Fortunately, the verses that soon followed were exactly what I was looking for.

"...'when seventy years are completed for Babylon, I will come to you and fulfill my gracious promise to bring you back to this place. For I know the plans I have for you,' declares the LORD, 'plans to prosper you and not to harm you, plans to give you a hope and a future. Then you will call upon Me and come and pray to Me, and I will listen to you. You will seek Me and find Me when you seek Me with all your heart. I will be found by you,' declares the Lord, 'and **will bring you back from captivity'**" (vs. 10-14).

The last words caused my heart to race. Was this my answer? In my mind, a little tug-of-war began as I tried to reason through what had just taken place. Was it coincidence I opened my Bible to those Scriptures or was it God who led me there? If it was God, why would He tell me to make myself at home if He really intended on getting me out? I felt both Scriptures were for me but how could this be since they seemed totally opposite?

Overwhelmed, I sat staring in a daze at the blood-splattered wall, trying to sort it all through. Finally, filled with frustration, I blurted out.

"Well, which is it, Lord? Are You going to get me out of here? Or should I make myself comfortable because I am going to stay awhile?"

At this, I paused once more to listen for a possible response but this time I didn't hear silence. Instead, I again heard that strange little voice trying to tell me I was talking to myself.

"And what about this?" I said ignoring it a second time while pointing to the Scripture.

"...seek the peace and prosperity of the city to which I carried you into exile. Pray to the LORD for it, because if it prospers, you too will prosper."

"Yeah, what about that anyway?" I wondered to myself. What exactly did this mean? After all, it seemed a puzzling concept to pray for the officers who got paid to terrorize us. At this thought, I actually burst out laughing but only to be quickly silenced when I heard a noise that brought me back to reality.

Down the hallway I heard a single voice crying amid all the noise. It was a woman calling for help.

"Please someone get a doctor! Officer call for help! I need medical!"

Her continual cries carried a sound of desperation to them. After a few minutes, some of the other prisoners even started calling for help on her behalf. Soon half a dozen inmates were kicking the metal doors, screaming for the guards to come but with no response. Then, because of all the noise they created, the rest of the inmates began to scream at them to shut up. Finally, after everyone raised quite a ruckus, the guards did show but not to give any assistance.

Instead, they took the situation as an opportunity for sport. As the sick woman continued to cry for medical attention, one of the officers responded by mocking her pleas.

"What's the matter? Do you need a doctor?" He whined in a pretend crybaby voice. "Are you going to die?" He asked, continuing to taunt her.

At this, all the guards burst into laughter. I could hear them advancing down the hallway, kicking doors and threatening as they went. But instead of intimidating the inmates to quiet down, it only caused them to clamor more because they were happy to get some kind of response after being ignored for so long.

The noise and confusion were now building in intensity. The sick woman's cries turned into screams. It was all too much. As I listened, I tried to suppress the anger rising up inside of me. Overwhelmed by the madness, I yelled in frustration, "Do something Lord, there must be a way to make this chaos stop!" Again, I heard no response. Still holding my Bible in my arms, my eyes looked down and landed on the same verse I just read minutes before.

"...seek the peace and prosperity of the city to which I have carried you into exile. Pray to the LORD for it, because if it prospers, you too will prosper."

As I read it again, I felt an intense stirring in me like something was urging me on, but to do what? *"Pray for it!"* I heard. Was God talking to me? I looked down again. That single word seemed to fill the page. ***"PRAY!"***

Suddenly, the realization hit me like a lightning bolt. I jumped up electrified. "OK, Lord," I said furiously pacing my little cell. "I don't know if I'm staying or going but while I am here I'm going to do what this says!" Right then I began to pray for those people outside my cell. I begged God to show them mercy. Asking Him to remove the drugs from their systems, ease their pain and flood them with peace. Then I prayed for the guards, rebuking the spirits of arrogance, mockery and hate and loosing on them the spirit of compassion. I also asked the Father to give those officers the heart of Jesus so they would want to help the inmates instead of harassing them. I prayed for the entire facility with fervency I never felt before. When I finally stopped, I realized it was quiet.

Stillness was over the block. As I listened, I thought to myself, "Wow, has everyone gone to sleep?" Obviously, I didn't know yet the power of prayer. In fact, I didn't even connect my prayer with what was happening until a few minutes later when the guards came back down the hall breaking the blessed silence.

As I walked over to my window, I was greeted with the sight of officers going cell to cell distributing blankets and mattresses. "It's about time." I thought as I watched the inmates collect them. Then I noticed a naive-looking man approaching one of the officers.

"I have a neck ache," I heard him say. "Do you think I can get an extra blanket to use as a pillow?"

When I heard this, I laughed to myself. "Fat chance buddy," I thought, waiting for the guard to slam the door in his face. But to my total surprise, the officer nodded his head in agreement and said, "Sure." as he handed the precious provision to the man.

I was astounded – an extra blanket? That was totally unheard of in this place. Still stunned, I watched the officers as they went back to each cell to make sure no one was missed. It was truly amazing, but only the beginning.

Thirty minutes later, the guards were back again. This time with sack lunches left over from earlier in the day. These were usually thrown out or eaten by the guards, but never given to the inmates. Now, here it was midnight and cookies and sandwiches were being divided amongst the cells.

Then, two minutes later, the impossible happened. Most of the prisoners were waiting to make a phone call but, as usual, their rights had been indefinitely delayed. Now one of the meanest guards, who was suddenly acting very friendly, opened up a cell and said,

"I can't take anyone out right now to make calls so I brought you the cordless phone from up front, go ahead and use it."

I heard myself gasp. Now this was too much. A woman in a cell across the hall from me was also watching everything transpire. She looked at me through the glass with wide-eyed amazement, and then shook her head as if to say, "I don't believe it!" I felt the same way. When I finally went to sleep, the only sounds I heard were the sounds of happy voices chattering on the phone.

I found out the next morning that everyone in that cell talked on the phone until they killed the battery. Several people got through to family, friends, or the bail bondsman, and then were released. I never found out if the woman who needed medical help ever got any, but I didn't hear her cry out anymore. The whole thing was so incredible it was downright spooky.

Two days later, I heard the magnetic lock being released on the door of my cell. I looked up as the head disciplinary officer stepped in. "Well, Ms. Caple, I have good news and I have bad news. Which do you want to hear first?"

"The bad." I said dryly.

"Well," he replied. "The bad news is it will take a couple of hours to process you out of here. The good news is you're going back to population."

My jaw must have dropped because I couldn't answer for a moment. Then incredulously I said,

"A couple of hours is not bad news, sir. Thank you."

Less than a half-hour later, I was strolling down the long hallway back to my unit. My 90-day administrative segregation flushed down the toilet. It was a miracle!!! What did Jeremiah's Scripture say? If I prayed for my place of exile and it prospered, I would prosper too!!! I felt like running down the hallway shouting, "This God-thing really works!!!" I was trembling. I could feel God's love and power. He showed me something incredible and it was just a taste of what was yet to come.

Lesson Ten

1. Describe an instance when, during your captivity, you experienced God moving in direct response to your prayers. Write down all the details you can remember about the event. Also, describe all the spiritual insights you received during it. Include any Scriptures the Lord gave you or any personal word He spoke into your spirit.

CHAPTER ELEVEN

PREPARATION FOR YOUR EXPECTED END

"And if they turn back to You with all their heart and soul in the land of their enemies who took them captive... then hear their prayer and their plea, and uphold their cause."
1 Kings 8:48-49

The Third of God's Purposes for Your Time from Solomon's Prayer

"*This is the text of the letter that the prophet Jeremiah sent from Jerusalem to the surviving elders among the exiles and to the priests, the prophets and all the other people Nebuchadnezzar had carried into exile from Jerusalem to Babylon. This is what the LORD Almighty, the God of Israel, says to all those I carried into exile from Jerusalem to Babylon: 'Build houses and settle down; plant gardens and eat what they produce. Marry and have sons and daughters; find wives for your sons and give your daughters in marriage, so that they too may have sons and daughters. Increase in number there; do not decrease. Also, seek the peace and prosperity of the city to which I have carried you into exile. Pray to the LORD for it, because if it prospers, you too will prosper...*" (Jeremiah 29:1, 4-7). **"For I know the thoughts that I think toward you, saith the Lord, thoughts of peace, and not of evil, to give you an Expected End"** (Jeremiah 29:11 KJV).

The first Scripture listed above is from Solomon's prayer. It is the third and final purpose God intends for your time. The next Scripture is from a letter sent to the ancient exiles who were imprisoned in Babylon. The reason why I put these Scriptures together is because what is contained in the letter is the way to fulfill the final purpose.

There are many books in the Bible that started out as a letter. Hebrews, Jude, and the New Testament epistles from Paul, are good examples. Paul's letters, interestingly enough, were written by him while he was being held captive in a Roman prison.

The second Scripture I listed above is from chapter 29 of Jeremiah entitled, *"A Letter to the Exiles."* This letter is unique because **it is the only one in the Bible God sent into prison.** Written by the prophet Jeremiah around 597 B.C., the letter was sent via a diplomatic pouch to the captives who were in Babylon. In it, under the inspiration and direction of the Holy Spirit, Jeremiah wrote a list of instructions for the captives to follow while they were in exile. At the end of the list was the promise of the future that God planned for each one of them. The instructions in the letter were designed to get the prisoners ready for this future.

God has a plan for you too! A unique purpose that will increase His Kingdom on Earth and bless your life greatly. This plan is called your *"Expected End."* The instructions in Jeremiah's letter are specifically designed to get you ready for it during your captivity. Look again at Solomon's prayer and learn the third purpose for your time:

"And if they turn back to You with all their heart and soul in the land of their enemies who took them captive... then hear their prayer and their plea, and uphold their cause."

How would you go about fulfilling this purpose? What does it take to turn back to God with all your heart and soul? **You must commit your entire life to Him and become what He created you to be.** Which means you must get prepared for and take possession of your Expected End.

While you are here, God wants to mold you into a perfectly formed instrument that He can use to build His Kingdom. God is on a mission to save the world. His plan is for you to go on this mission with Him. Now is the time for you to get ready to join God in His work. This is the final purpose God wants done during your time. It is the biggest reason why He brought you into captivity. To get you prepared for your future assignment!

This is what Jeremiah's letter is all about - preparation. The reason God sent the letter to His people in Babylonia was so they could use their time inside to get ready for His Kingdom purposes. The Bible contains many examples of God using a person's captivity as a vehicle to train them for their assignment.

Joseph spent 13 years in prison preparing to become second-in-command over all of Egypt and to save the world from famine! The apostle Paul wrote his letters while in prison, which today touch millions of people around the world! Plus, there were six other prisoners in the Bible, all from the Babylonian exile, who took possession of their Expected End through the vehicle of their captivity.

Daniel, during his exile, received the training he needed to become Babylon's third-highest ruler and the foremost prophet of Christ's coming in the end times!

Esther, while a prisoner in the king's palace, went through a year of preparation to become queen. When she took the throne, the slaughter of all the Israelites left in the land of captivity was stopped!

Zerubbabel and Jeshua were still in Babylon when they received their assignment to go to Jerusalem to rebuild Solomon's burned down temple!

Ezra faithfully studied the Scriptures during his captivity. By the time he was released to go home, he was ready to teach the Word of God to the returned exiles!

Nehemiah was acting as the king's cupbearer in the land of captivity when he received his assignment to go to Jerusalem to rebuild the broken-down walls!

For a bunch of ex-cons, this is quite a list of accomplishments! How did they do it? These six captives were all related in a very specific way. All were products of the Babylonian exile, so all read Jeremiah's letter, which enabled them to take possession of their Expected End!

The directions in Jeremiah's letter are designed to get you ready for your assignment. Throughout the years of my incarceration I lived out these instructions. I am now the founder of Expected End Ministries! When followed, these guidelines work! This is why we are going to spend the next few chapters going through the letter. I am going to show you how to directly apply its instructions to your captivity, so you can be prepared to possess your future mission.

Now, I want to emphasize an important point. Taking possession of your Expected End is one of God's purposes for your time, so you must have it in order for the chastisement of your captivity to end. Do you remember the warning Jeremiah made concerning this? *"[Their chastisement will continue until it has accomplished its purpose]..."* (Jeremiah 4:22 AMP).

God wants certain purposes accomplished during your time. The last one is to get you prepared to possess your Expected End. Why would the chastisement of your captivity continue if you didn't fulfill this purpose? Your Expected End is the only thing that can enable you to be free whether you are inside or out. Having possession of it will cause you to be filled with hope and supernatural joy! It will enable you to endure any situation and overcome any temptation! It will also empower you to do your time with purpose and ensure your success upon your release.

The benefits of possessing your Expected End are endless and **powerful.** Powerful enough to radically change your life while you are here plus **ensure you don't ever come back into captivity once you leave.** This is why you must take possession of your Expected End now. It is the only thing that can bring the cycle of your captivity to an end!

While I was in prison, I got prepared for and took possession of my Expected End. Having my created purpose completely changed the way I did the rest of my time. I was constantly filled with excitement because of the awesome future God was preparing for me! The supernatural joy I received from walking out my assignment made my days fly by. In fact, there were times when it didn't even seem like I was in prison.

Once I got out, then continued to pursue my mission, the benefits of possessing my Expected End were made even more apparent. Empowered with my purpose, I was never tempted to go back to dope or to slip back into my old ways. Having my assignment set a fire blazing inside of me that enabled me to overcome any obstacles.

Plus, I was supernaturally surrounded by favor everywhere I went. Countless blessings were poured out on me because I was pursuing my created purpose!

Unfortunately, other ex-cons I knew weren't doing so well. They were struggling through their daily existence. Many violated probation and went back to prison. **Even the Christians who were pursuing God were going back!** Why? They didn't have possession of the only thing that could keep them from failing and ensure their success. Their Expected End!

This is why God insists that you get your Expected End while you are here. It is the **ONLY** thing that can bring total satisfaction to your life, prevent you from going back to your old ways, and **give you the life you've always dreamed of!** God wants you to live abundantly. Possessing your assignment will ensure you do!

You must use your time here to get ready for your assignment. The next three chapters of this study are of vital importance to your future. So, don't just read them, put what you learn into practice. If you don't, you will never experience the inheritance God has for you - your land flowing with milk and honey.

Lesson Eleven

1. This is Solomon's third and final purpose for your time. *"And if they turn back to You with all their heart and soul in the land of their enemies who took them captive... then hear their prayer and their plea and uphold their cause"* (1 Kings 8:48-49). How would you go about fulfilling this purpose?

2. Write out Jeremiah 29:11.

3. The rest of your captivity should be spent preparing for your Expected End. It is vitally important that you get equipped for your God-created purpose now, while you are still in captivity. Doing so will determine whether you experience life in its fullness or return to captivity again. Name three ancient Israelite captives who were trained for their Expected End during their captivity. List their accomplishments.

4. Do you believe those people could have completed their missions if they hadn't been prepared during their captivity? Why?

CHAPTER TWELVE

"This is what the LORD Almighty, the God of Israel, says to all those I carried into exile from Jerusalem to Babylon: 'Build houses and settle down; plant gardens and eat what they produce."

Jeremiah 29:4-5.

"For I know the thoughts that I think toward you, saith the LORD, thoughts of peace, and not of evil, to give you an Expected End."
Jeremiah 29:11 KJV

The first instruction in Jeremiah's letter tied to the promise of your Expected End is this: *"Build houses and settle down."* You must start preparing yourself to possess your Expected End by building your house. So how do you begin? The letter itself tells you. The only way to correctly *"build houses"* is to *"settle down"* into a Christ-centered lifestyle. What does this mean?

To live Christ-centered is to have a total dependence on God. To know you need His wisdom and presence to guide you through each day. The way you walk this out is by regularly seeking God through Bible study, prayer and meditation. Settling into this kind of a Christ-centered lifestyle is how you build your house. **Spending personal time with God everyday is the first discipline you need in order to be successful for the rest of your life.** This is why it is the first instruction in Jeremiah's letter.

Choosing to settle down into a Christ-centered lifestyle means you will need to make right decisions on how to spend your time while you're inside. Will you involve yourself in the things of the world or the things of God? Scripture says,

"...But each one should be careful how he builds. For no one can lay any foundation other than the one already laid, which is Jesus Christ. If any man builds on this foundation using gold, silver, costly stones, wood, hay or straw, his work will be shown for what it is, because the Day will bring it to light. It will be revealed with fire, and the fire will test the quality of each man's work. If what he has built survives, he will receive his reward" (1 Corinthians 3:10-14).

You are now building for your future. Christ is the foundation your dream house stands on. This means you must build the rest of your house with materials that come from Him. When you use the right building blocks, like prayer and study of the Word, your house will stand firm through every fiery trial. If you choose, however, to build with things the world has to offer, your house will be destroyed.

During my time inside, I made a commitment to put God as my number One priority. When it came to choosing between reading my Bible and praying versus playing cards and watching TV, I put God first by choosing to read and pray. Don't get me wrong; there were moments when I indulged in those other kinds of activities, but I always made sure the majority of my time was spent pursuing God.

As a result, I am now running a highly successful ministry, but let me tell you, my success didn't just happen. It came from years of living Christ-centered. Do you believe you can build for your future by playing spades and watching soaps all day? No. On the contrary, your future success will depend heavily on your commitment to studying God's Word and spending time with Him. There are a lot of other activities available in prison to distract you from living Christ-centered. The question is: are you going to let those distractions rob you of your future dreams? God doesn't want you to eliminate all the recreation in your life. He wants you to have fun and lots of it. However, He also wants you to use your time of captivity wisely, studying and getting prepared for your call. This means eliminating anything hindering your growth.

Unfortunately, most people consider activities involving God to be boring. After all, what could possibly be exciting about praying or reading the Bible? Well, if you feel this way you haven't truly tasted life with God because, if you did, you would be hooked! My life is so exciting because I live a Christ-centered existence! Having a deep personal relationship with my Lord is like going on a great adventure. He constantly amazes me! I am always in anticipation to see what He will do next!

One of the greatest things living Christ-centered does is to help you develop your ear to hear God and your heart to obey. As you sit in the presence of the Lord through prayer, Bible study, worship or meditation, He will give you supernatural knowledge and guidance that, when followed, will usher His miraculous power into your life. Let me give you a small example.

I remember an occasion, while at a prayer meeting, I was asked to pray for an inmate's mother. After being examined by her doctors, this woman was scheduled for heart surgery because there were numerous blood clots blocking her arteries. I began my prayer by asking the Lord to guide the surgeon's hands during the operation. Immediately, however, God impressed upon me that I was praying in the wrong direction. He said not to pray for the surgeon but, instead, to pray specifically for the blood clots to be dissolved. So I did. The next day the group received the report that the surgery was canceled because, during the pre-operative check, the doctors discovered the clots were no longer there. They completely disappeared!

Jesus prayed for God's Kingdom to come and His will be done on earth as it is in heaven. (Matthew 6:10) How do you think God goes about accomplishing His will on earth? He does it through us! Being able to hear from God is very important because it enables you to do what He specifically wills! Let me tell you what would have happened if I continued to pray for that woman in my own wisdom. Nothing, that's what!

There are so many reasons why I love being able to hear from God. He is my Friend who will tell me when I am sinning against Him or hurting other people and myself. He guides me when I have a crucial decision to make. He leads me away from danger and toward my destiny. When I live Christ-centered, God directs the path of my life to His Glory and my advantage.

There are a lot of people walking around saying they are Christians; but, because they are not living a Christ-centered existence, they have none of God's power accompanying their claim. You see, the more time you spend with God in His Word and in prayer, the more He will change and empower you. There was a time in prison when I was praying with three different groups a day plus my own meditation time. This is a lot of praying! The result was that I came closer to God. In turn, He gave me an increased anointing to enable me to pray with more effectiveness.

One night at a prayer circle, a sister who was very skeptical in things of the supernatural nature told me she was perplexed about a phenomenon she was experiencing. It seemed whenever the group would meet and I happened to be standing next to her, something unusual would take place. As I prayed, she would get major goose bumps but only on one side of her body, the side where I was holding her hand. In fact, she said the difference she felt between her one side and the other was so distinct it was as though a dividing line was drawn down the length of her body, splitting it in half. On the side I was holding her hand, she got chills but, on the other side, she had none. This phenomenon lasted only while I was praying. When I finished, it stopped.

I'm not telling you this to boast, but to make a point. This didn't happen because I was more spiritual than anyone else, but rather because I was spending a lot of time with God in prayer. So, in turn, He was making sure I possessed the power to get those prayers answered! God empowers you when you are living Christ-centered. Do you want to effectively carry out God's work? If so, you must cling to Him daily by communing with Him and searching His Scriptures.

When I got out of prison, I continued in my daily discipline of living Christ-centered. Because of this, I was abundantly blessed in every area of my life. Unfortunately, every other ex-felon I knew was struggling to make it. In fact, most were sent back to the joint. So, what was the difference between them and me? Two things: Daily, I practiced living Christ-centered and I had possession of my Expected End.

I need to stop right here to make a very important point. The main focus of this book is to get you prepared to possess your Expected End. **However, Christ-centered**

living is more important than your assignment and must always come first! This is why it is the first instruction in Jeremiah's letter. It is the foundational building block necessary for you to possess your assignment! Without a close relationship with the Lord, you won't be able to hear His direction concerning your mission. Without daily study and prayer, you won't have the tools you need to minister effectively while you are walking out your assignment. Without a daily dependence on God, you will fail in your mission because you'll be walking in your own limited strength instead of His unlimited power!

About a year and a half after I got out, I briefly fell into a pattern of not reading and praying every day. I was very busy at the time writing this study, working a full-time job, being a wife, spending time with my family and keeping my new home in order. However, because I continued to work on *The Captivity Series* on a daily basis, I justified that I didn't need to study. After all, I was still doing a "God" thing. Well, a few months later, the Lord let me know He didn't consider working on my Expected End a substitute for my daily personal time with Him. He also made it clear that, if I didn't go back to putting my habit of living Christ-centered first, my ability to do my assignment would suffer.

We must be careful about what things we start substituting for our personal relationship with God. Christian novels aren't bad, neither are Christian TV or activities. Unfortunately, any of these things can become dangerous when we let them replace our daily one-on-one time with God.

Here is one last point for those of you who are already living Christ-centered. You need to pay attention to this chapter because it is easy to get overconfident when you've already developed a daily discipline of prayer and study. Trust me when I say that, though you might be doing well now, each new day will present an opportunity for you to slip in your practice. This is especially true when you get out. You will be so busy you will think you don't have time to pray or read. However, when this happens, remember to make time because your life, survival and future will depend upon it.

Strive to spend your time here wisely. Consider your incarceration as Bible College, a time to study and grow. God instructed you to *"build houses and settle down"* because it is the only way to ensure lasting success for the rest of your life.

Now, let's go back to look again at the first verse from Jeremiah's letter. *"Build houses and settle down, **plant gardens and eat what they produce**..."* The second half of this verse contains an instruction connected to a promise. The instruction says to *"plant gardens"* while you are in exile because, if you do, you will get to *"eat what they produce."*

So, how do you plant a garden while you are in prison? Well, if you look at the whole verse again you will see that building your house and planting your garden go together. The instruction to plant is directly connected with settling down into a Christ-centered lifestyle. Every time you choose to do the things of God you are planting seeds into your garden.

You see, each time you speak out a Scripture over your family, you plant a seed in their life. Every time you pray for your future assignment, you are planting a seed into your future. Any time you serve someone, you are planting a seed. Any time you read the Word, you are planting a seed. The list goes on and on. Every time you do something to live Christ-centered, you are planting seeds in your garden, which will one day produce a harvest that, the Scripture promises, you will be able to feast from!

Let's look at how this process works by studying the law of sowing and reaping. God has established laws by which the universe is run. The law of gravity is one of them. Gravity is constant. You will never float off into space because gravity is always working to hold you down on the earth. This is how the law of sowing and reaping is. It is constant. It never changes and it always works. Let us investigate how this law operates by starting with the first part – sowing.

"Do not be deceived: God cannot be mocked. A man reaps what he sows" (Galatians 6:7).

The law of sowing guarantees whatever you plant is what you will harvest. Example: If you were to sow a kernel of corn you would not get back watermelon, you would get back corn. God's law of sowing works like this every time with everything, including the things of the spirit.

The second part of the law of sowing and reaping is you will always harvest more than you plant! Let me explain. If you put one kernel of corn in the ground, it will grow a stalk with an average of six ears of corn, each ear with 100 or more kernels. This means you get **600** kernels of corn harvested from just the **one** seed planted. What an incredible increase! It is one of God's laws of the universe so **the increase is always guaranteed.** This is why God instructed you to *"plant gardens"* while you are in exile because His law of sowing and reaping guarantees you an abundant harvest if you do.

Did you know one of Webster's meanings to the word *gardens* is "a well-cultivated region; area of fertile, developed land." This means God in His grace and mercy made sure the ground in your captivity is well cultivated and fertile. Why? So that those who choose to plant while they are in exile will be rewarded with an extraordinary harvest. Look at what Psalm 126 says about this.

"When the Lord brought back the captives to Zion, we were like men who dreamed. Our mouths were filled with laughter, our tongues were songs of joy. Then it was said among the nations, 'The Lord has done great things for them.' The Lord has done great things for us, and we are filled with joy. Those who sow in tears will reap with songs of

joy. He who goes out weeping, carrying seed to sow, will return with songs of joy, carrying sheaves with him" (vs. 1-3, 5-6).

The ancient captives of Babylon wrote this Psalm when they returned to Jerusalem after their years in exile. In it, they share how unreal it felt to be home. How God did such great things for them through their captivity that even the other nations recognized they were blessed. In this verse, the exiles tell us the secret as to how they received all those blessings.

"He who goes out weeping, carrying seed to sow, will return with songs of joy, carrying sheaves with him." Because the exiles obeyed Jeremiah's instructions to plant gardens while they were in captivity, they were reaping what those gardens produced! In fact, the Israelites' harvest from captivity was so great **they were already carrying bundles of it before they arrived in the land flowing with milk and honey!**

While I was in prison, I planted seed everywhere. I prayed for my family. I spoke Scriptures over my life. I released seeds of faith into my future. Since being released, I've received such a huge harvest everyone around me continues to marvel at what God is doing in my life! Like ancient Israel, I've been blessed in more ways than I can count. I am literally feasting on the banquet my garden is producing!

God wants your harvest to be abundant too, but for this to happen you must plant seed. Seed in prayer for your future, seed in the Word, seed in service to God. Remember His law of sowing and reaping is **guaranteed,** which means it possesses unlimited potential! The only thing that can put a cap on it is you. Think carefully – the size of your harvest depends on you and the amount of seed you plant. The more seed you plant, the bigger your harvest.

Now, let me warn about what will happen when you decide to follow these instructions to build and plant. Your enemy, satan, is painfully aware of the guaranteed harvest promised to you in Jeremiah's letter. The last thing he wants is for you to obey its instructions. Beware! He will try every dirty trick in the book to get you to miss out on sowing seed in your life. All kinds of problems, from subtle, to full frontal attacks will arise as you try to develop your habit of Christ-centered living. You will suddenly become sleepy when you read your Bible. The enemy will use another person to distract you from your walk. He will even stir up a fierce disagreement between you and another Christian to get you to stop going to prayer, choir or church. These attacks are from the enemy who creates situations to get you to stop sowing seed. Do not fall for it! When you fail to continue doing the things of God because of other people or circumstances, you have fallen for one of satan's oldest tricks. So, don't let him succeed in robbing you of your harvest.

Next, be careful what you plant. Remember whatever seed you use, good or bad, is what you are going to harvest a lot of. If you are planting the things of God, you will be blessed; but if you are planting the things of the world, you will reap a harvest of misery and bitter fruit. The Bible says;

"Do not be deceived: God cannot be mocked. A man reaps what he sows. The one who sows to please his sinful nature, from that nature will reap destruction; the one who sows to please the Spirit, from the Spirit will reap eternal life" (Galatians 6:7-8).

When you sow into the Spirit, you will reap the blessings God stores up for you in the spiritual realm. However, when you sow things from your sinful nature, like pride, greed, gossip, criticism, anger or laziness, you are going to reap the fruit those behaviors bring. So, make sure your seed is good or your harvest will be abundantly bad.

Lastly, you need to know there is always a period of waiting between the time you plant and the time you harvest. Think about it. If you planted a seed in the ground right now, would you stand over it expecting a plant to immediately spring up? No, this would be ridiculous! Don't be too impatient to see a harvest, because every seed takes time to germinate. There will always be a period of waiting. Unfortunately, most people give up during this time. They fall away from doing the things of God because they aren't seeing any results. Galatians 6:9 says,

"Let us not become weary in doing good, for at the proper time we will reap a harvest if we do not give up."

From the very beginning of my incarceration, I sowed seed all over the place, but, at first, nothing happened. Sometimes, I felt like giving up; but, because I continued to do the good things of God, my harvest arrived and did not stop! In fact, on my best day, I could never dream up the blessings I've received. So hold on! Do not quit! Build and plant while you are here, then get ready to receive your harvest.

Lesson Twelve

1. The instructions contained in Jeremiah's letter are meant to get you prepared for your Expected End. The first instruction: *"This is what the LORD Almighty, the God of Israel, says to all those I carried into exile from Jerusalem to Babylon: 'Build houses and settle down; plant gardens and eat what they produce..."* (Jeremiah 29:4-5). *"For I know the thoughts that I think towards you,' saith the Lord, 'thoughts of peace and not of evil, to give you an Expected End'"* (Jeremiah 29:11 KJV). How do you start building your house while you are in captivity?

2. Name different things you can do to settle into a Christ-centered lifestyle while you are inside.

3. Name different ways you can *"plant gardens"* while you are in captivity.

4. If you choose to be obedient to Jeremiah's instruction to *"plant gardens"* while you are in captivity the Scripture says you will be able to "_____ what they produce." (Fill in the blank.) What does this mean to you?

5. Explain the law of sowing and reaping. How does this law benefit those who choose to obey Jeremiah's instruction to *"plant gardens"* while in captivity?

CHAPTER THIRTEEN

"Marry and have sons and daughters; find wives for your sons and give your daughters in marriage, so that they too may have sons and daughters. Increase in number there; do not decrease."
Jeremiah 29:6

"For I know the thoughts that I think toward you, saith the Lord, thoughts of peace, and not of evil to give you an Expected End."
Jeremiah 29:11 KJV

The second instruction in Jeremiah's letter tied to the promise of your Expected End directs you to build family while you are in exile. What exactly does God mean by *family*? Webster's dictionary defines *family* as: "fellowship, a group of people united by certain convictions (as of religion or philosophy)."

Family is fellowship, the body of Christ gathering together, studying the Scriptures, worshiping God, and serving Him and other people. This is what God wants you to be a part of while you are inside because your involvement in the body helps prepare you for your Expected End. This is why the instruction to build the family is followed by the promise of your future.

"Marry and have sons and daughters... increase in number there; do not decrease... For I know the plans I have for you, declares the Lord, plans to give you a hope and a future... to give you an Expected End."

The command to build family and the promise of an Expected End are virtually back-to-back because they are intricately tied together. It is during your involvement in the fellowship that you will receive the on-the-job training you must get to be qualified for your future assignment. Only in the body can you learn skills and the vital lessons needed to walk out your created purpose.

Joseph is the perfect biblical example of someone who received training for his Expected End while being active within a group of people in prison. The Bible says during his captivity, *"...the warden put Joseph in charge of all those held in the prison..."* (Genesis 39:22).

Joseph's job in captivity directly involved him with his fellow inmates. For 13 years, he managed, distributed and supervised all of the other prisoners' needs. What did Joseph's participation in this "family" do for him? It polished and perfected his skills; the same skills he would later use to manage, distribute, and supervise the grain stores, which saved the entire country during a famine! Joseph was placed as second-in-command over Egypt because **he was qualified for the job.** That is why you must become active in the fellowship in your prison, because your participation will qualify you for your future assignment.

Looking back, I can see how God used my activity in the prison fellowship to train me for this ministry. It all began in county jail where I started Bible studies in my cell with two people. Quickly the group grew to 10, which were too many to fit in my cell, so I moved the study out into the pod. There, I began instructing, praying with all the women, leading new commits to Christ, and leading everyone in worship.

As our little "family" grew and I functioned as the leader over the body, my knowledge and skills increased, enabling me to take on even more responsibility. Eventually, the chaplain of the facility asked me to conduct Bible studies across the hallway, which meant I was able to teach all the female units, not just my own.

The next step in my training came when I was transported to federal prison. Within nine months after my arrival, God led four other sisters and me to start a ministry. Once again, I began teaching Bible studies and leading worship, but on a much bigger scale. Because I needed to constantly study and go before the Lord in receiving guidance in handling a larger ministry, my abilities were greatly increased. Eventually my skills were fine-tuned to the point where I was ready for this present-day ministry! You see, just like Joseph, God used my activity in the body to prepare me for my Expected End.

Through God's plan, many other women also benefited from their involvement in this same ministry. When I first arrived in prison, there were a small number of serious Christians scattered around the compound. Though each one of them was living a Christ-centered lifestyle, building houses and planting gardens, they were doing it apart from a body of believers.

One night the Lord corrected this situation by giving five of us, who barely knew each other, the same idea to start a Christian fellowship. Four days later, we gathered for what would become our monthly fellowship party. Fifty women showed up! Immediately, God took what were a few scattered Christians and turned us into a body of believers.

As the ministry continued to grow, we added more activities like an additional Bible study, a system of tithing to help out new commits, and a corporate prayer team to pray for the facility. Having these new sub-ministries provided added opportunities for the women to get directly involved in the fellowship and to receive the necessary training for their future assignments. Some women who chose to be active in it are now on the streets using their experience to attain their dreams!

Unfortunately, many people today are negligent in getting involved in their prison fellowship. In fact, there is an epidemic level of division and isolation in the inmate population, even amongst the Christians. Well, let me warn you, this division is more dangerous than a deadly virus. If it infects you, it could literally rob you of your future. I've heard a lot of excuses from inmates about why they do not attend fellowship.

One of them is "I have my own relationship with God." That statement implies a lack of knowledge on the absolute importance that God places on fellowship. Inmates who do not understand the principle of getting involved in the body will miss out on the training they need to be prepared for their Expected End. Imagine what would have happened if Joseph decided to do his time alone and not be active amongst his fellow prisoners. When the opportunity came for him to apply for the position as head over Egypt, he wouldn't have gotten the job because he wouldn't have been qualified!

Those who believe they need to do their time with God and God alone miss out on the exciting ways God wants to use them within the fellowship. I remember a time when I was with a group of Spanish women who were praying. There was a request from someone who needed healing. Ten minutes after we started to pray, I heard the Lord speak to me. He told me to reach over and lay my hand on the woman, so I did. When I touched her, something like electricity started shooting back and forth across my rib cage. The whole experience lasted less than a minute, during which time I said nothing. I just kept my hand on her until the "electricity" stopped, and then I removed it. She was healed. In fact, another woman who was standing next to her was healed of chronic backaches at the same time because she inadvertently touched the first women when God's healing power was being released!

Let me tell you why this happened. First, because I spent so much time with the Lord, I recognized His voice when He spoke. **Second, it happened because I was there being active in the body.** My mere presence gave the opportunity for God to use me to activate His healing power. Trust me when I tell you that, if you are consistently faithful in your participation in the fellowship, God will use you just because you are there.

The second most frequent excuse I hear from inmates who don't fellowship is: "I don't go to church because of all the hypocrites who are there." Unfortunately, people who do not attend fellowship for this reason, in reality, have a problem themselves. More often than not, these are the ones who can be difficult. That is another reason why you need to be active in the body, so you can become aware of weaknesses in your own behavior toward others.

Strife and division amongst the body is its biggest enemy. These things are usually caused by character flaws within us, not other people. When you stay isolated from others, your character flaws also stay hidden, poisoning yourself and sabotaging your future. As you function within the family you will begin to discover just how judgmental you can be, how quick you are to gossip, or how prideful you can act. The more active you are in the body, the more situations will arise to expose these kinds of behaviors.

Author Elisabeth Elliot makes a thought-provoking statement about this in her book, *"A Slow and Certain Light."* She writes, "God isolates a man in order to reveal Himself. It is alone that a man most clearly recognizes God for who He is. **But it is in relationship with his fellow men that he comes to know himself. Seeking the will of God as though it had nothing to do with anybody else leads to all kinds of distortions."**

Mrs. Elliot points out two powerful truths. First, it takes being involved with people for you to get to know what is going on inside yourself. Second, God's will for your life will always involve other people. This is why you must learn to deal with them in a godly manner.

Whatever your Expected End, it will involve people. God is in the business of saving people. In fact, He sent His only Son to die for us; so, obviously, people are His number one priority. There will be many times in your life and during your assignment in which you will be required to deal with someone who possesses far from perfect behavior.

However, think about this. If they were perfect, they wouldn't need your help! As Jesus said, it is the sick that need a doctor, not those who are well (Matthew 9:12). You need to go to fellowship even if there is someone there you can't stand. **Then you need to change your attitude about that person and start loving them as God loves you, faults and all!** It is easy to love people who are already loveable. Your challenge and your growth will come when you learn to embrace someone who is difficult, trying and obnoxious. Remember, in your dream job, you will always be required to work with less than dreamy people.

So far, we have looked at some very important reasons why getting involved in the body is essential for you. Now, I would be remiss if I didn't show you one last principle concerning the "family." This biblical truth is vitally important because it will dramatically affect your future financial stability.

You know as well as I do that lack of money is what drove many of us to choose crime as a way of life. However, because we tried to acquire financial freedom through our criminal activities, we ended up in captivity. Do you want this to happen again?

Envision being comfortable, plus, having all your needs met, and even prospering in abundance. How can this happen? Well, for one, Jesus promised it (Matthew 6:24-34).

Also, the Scriptures say that **through your activity in the body you will be prospered.**

Let me show you proof of this from the book of Psalms.

"God places the solitary in families and gives the desolate a home in which to dwell; He leads the prisoners out to prosperity; but the rebellious dwell in a parched land" (Psalm 68:6 AMP).

God wants to place solo Christians within His family because it is there in the fellowship that He ***"leads the prisoners out to prosperity."*** How does this work? A famous preacher named Mike Murdock once said, "Your prosperity lies in your assignment!" By this, he meant that as long as you are pursuing your Expected End, God will providentially see to all your needs, both Kingdom and personal. Why would God do this? Because only when you are free from financial worry can you fully concentrate and complete the job He assigned to you.

Think about it. Do you believe you could really put all your attention into pursuing your mission if you were constantly worried about paying your rent? Do you think you could complete your mission if you didn't have all the finances you needed to do so? God provides for His people who are pursuing their Expected End so they will be freed up to complete His work. However, there is the catch: **In order to be qualified to possess your assignment you must first be trained within the body!** This is why the psalmist said God prospers you **through your placement in the family.**

While I was in prison, I was trained for this mission through my position in the fellowship. When I got out of prison, I continued to work on my Expected End and there was not a single day my husband and I couldn't financially meet all of our obligations. In fact, for the first year after our release, even though we worked at average paying jobs, we were three months ahead on our bills, driving new cars, and living very comfortably in our own home. How did this happen? God supernaturally prospered us **because we were following after our purpose!**

Five months after we moved into our house, the Lord directed my husband to start his own business. I will never forget the night God spoke to Bobby about his new company. My husband came into the living room still dripping wet from the shower, looking wide-eyed. He repeated the words the Lord told him. **"I am going to increase your business so that she can be about My business!"**

When my husband said it, I became so electrified it felt as though I was struck by lightning! God was proving His Scriptural promise to provide for those who were pursuing their assignments. He was going to financially increase my husband's business so I could be freed up to pursue His business: my Expected End!

Immediately, Bobby's company took off, bringing in three times more money in just one day than he previously made in a week. This eventually enabled me to quit my full time job to get "Expected End Ministries" going full time! Trust me when I tell you that God will always finance His people who are doing His projects. However, don't forget this: **The only reason I was qualified to do my assignment was because of the training I received in the body of believers while I was in prison!**

Your future prosperity lies in your Expected End. You must get prepared for your assignment by getting involved in the body. The Scripture from Psalms says you will prosper through your placement in the family, but the same verse also gives a warning to those who don't get involved, *"but the rebellious dwell in a parched land."* This parched land is the place of no provisions, spiritual or otherwise. It is what your future will hold if you do not get active in the body now.

Getting involved is easy! Just join in and offer up your God-given gifts. Are you developing your prayer skills? Now go and pray for someone. Do you possess administrative or help skills? Offer to help the body get organized. Are you studying God's Word? Teach a Bible study. Is there no existing fellowship? Start one. The opportunities are endless, but you must go and pursue them. When you do, you will find the "family" is the place where you will be prepared for your dreams!

Lesson Thirteen

1. The instructions in Jeremiah's letter are meant to prepare you for your Expected End. The second instruction: *"Marry and have sons and daughters; find wives for your sons and give your daughters in marriage, so that they too may have sons and daughters. Increase in number there; do not decrease"* (Jeremiah 29:6). *"For I know the thoughts that I think towards you, saith the LORD, thoughts of peace, and not of evil, to give you an Expected End"* (Jeremiah 29:11 KJV). God wants you to be involved in building the family of God while you are in captivity. Why is it so important for you to be involved in a fellowship?

2. What person in the Bible was trained for their Expected End within a group of inmates? What did that person end up doing?

3. How will your involvement in the body help prepare you for your Expected End? List as many reasons as possible.

4. If any, list the reasons why you might have hesitated to get involved in the body.

5. Mike Murdock once said, "Your prosperity lies in your assignment!" By this he meant that as long as you are pursuing your Expected End, God will providentially see to all your needs and obligations. Are you able to find encouragement in this? If so, in what ways?

CHAPTER FOURTEEN

"Also, seek the peace and prosperity of the city to which I have carried you into exile. Pray to the LORD for it, because if it prospers, you too will prosper."
Jeremiah 29:7

"For I know the thoughts that I think toward you, saith the LORD, thoughts of peace, and not of evil, to give you an Expected End."
Jeremiah 29:11 KJV

This is the last of God's commands in Jeremiah's letter connected to the promise of your Expected End. The instruction directs you to pray for your place of captivity because, if it prospers, you will prosper too. For the ancient Israelite captives, this was an unprecedented idea. Never before were they told to pray for the prosperity of their enemies, much less the ones who were holding them captive. Yet, here was God's surprising command to do so – why?

Prayer changes things. It bids provisions stored in heaven to come to earth. It moves the hand of God to move in your situation. Imagine possessing the ability to change the entire prison system. Well, you don't have to imagine because it can happen through prayer!

I will never forget the last time I was in lockdown. God revealed to me the power He would make available to those who would pray for their facility. I will also never forget being miraculously released from serving 90 days in the hole because I obeyed Jeremiah's instructions. What happened to me in booking can happen to you and your prison. It is that simple! When God says He will bring peace and prosperity to both you and your facility, He means it. You must, however pray in order for it to happen.

Unfortunately, very few prisoners have tapped into this truth. In fact, most do more complaining about their facility than praying for it. I believe if we spent the same amount of time on our knees praying as we do griping, we would be shocked at the results! We would experience an outpouring of God's blessing on our prisons as never witnessed before!

In this chapter, I am going to show you proof from the book of Daniel that praying for your facility will cause both you and your prison to prosper. The entire book of Daniel takes place in Babylon. In 605 B.C., Daniel was taken to Babylon in the first deportation of captives from Jerusalem. Can you imagine how he felt as he walked almost 1,000 miles in chains to prison? Daniel was only a young man. His world had been turned upside down. At that time, he did not even realize the awesome things

God was about to do for him through his exile. In fact, Daniel prospered so much while he was in Babylon that, if you didn't know better, you wouldn't have believed he was an inmate!

When Daniel first arrived in Babylon, he was taken to the palace to be trained in the service of King Nebuchadnezzar. Immediately, God blessed Daniel with all kinds of wisdom and knowledge, and then began giving him favor with the palace officials. Soon, Daniel was promoted to ruler of the province of Babylon and chief governor over its wise men!

Through the years, as Daniel's abilities continued to grow, so did his status. He was lavished with honor, gifts, and respect as he skyrocketed to higher and higher positions within Babylon. His second promotion came when Nebuchadnezzar's successor, Belshazzar, made Daniel third-highest ruler in the kingdom. Then Belshazzar's successor, Darius, eventually set him over the whole realm! Imagine that, Daniel in charge of the very land where he was being held captive. Not bad for an inmate!

Even in times of total persecution and extreme mortal danger, the Scriptures say Daniel came through without a scratch. What was his secret? How did Daniel prosper so greatly while locked up in prison? The answer is **prayer**. Daniel 6:10 says, *"...Three times a day he got down on his knees and prayed, giving thanks to his God, just as he had done before."*

Daniel was a committed man of prayer. But what did Daniel pray? In Chapter Eight of this study, we learned Daniel prayed for God to forgive the prisoners and release them from their captivity. But for what else was Daniel praying? According to what we can deduce from Scripture, he was praying for Babylon, the place where he was in exile. Daniel 9:2 says, *"...I, Daniel, understood from the Scriptures, according to the word of the LORD given to Jeremiah the prophet, that the desolation of Jerusalem would last seventy years."*

This information about the *seventy years* comes directly from Jeremiah's *Letter to the Exiles*, where it says, *"...when seventy years are completed for Babylon, I will come to you and fulfill my gracious promise to bring you back to this place"* (Jeremiah 29:10).

What this proves is that Daniel read Jeremiah's letter. The very same one you and I are studying today! Since Daniel was a true man of God, we can safely assume he not only read the letter, but also obeyed its instructions. This includes the instruction to pray for his place of exile. Scripture says, *"three times a day he got down on his knees and prayed,"* and because of that, Babylon flourished and so did he.

Let's look at the heights of prosperity experienced by Babylon during the Israelite captivity. History tells us the Neo-Babylonian Empire carried out a massive building program, which produced one of the largest, wealthiest cities in the ancient world.

Babylon covered 500 acres of land. It was encircled by a protective wall so thick a four-horse chariot could make a full turn on top of it. The wall contained 100 gates and entryways, many lined with colossal gold statues, decorative lions, and dragons. Babylon boasted of over 1,000 temples, including a 300-foot ziggurat (tiered-like) stadium. The city also contained the famed hanging gardens, which are called one of the Seven Wonders of the Ancient World!

Babylon's phenomenal prosperity wasn't just luck. It was God prospering the city because His captive people were praying for it. It was prayer warriors like Daniel that ushered in the wealth of Babylon. In fact, when Nebuchadnezzar, King of Babylon, tried to take credit for Babylon's prosperity, God put him in check. The Scripture says,

"...as the king was walking on the roof of the royal palace of Babylon, he said, 'Is not this the great Babylon I have built as the royal residence, by my mighty power and for the glory of my majesty?' The words were still on his lips when a voice came from heaven, 'This is what is decreed for you, King Nebuchadnezzar: Your royal authority has been taken from you. You will be driven away from people and will live with the wild animals; you will eat grass like cattle. Seven times will pass by for you until you acknowledge that the Most High is sovereign over the kingdoms of men and gives them to anyone he wishes.' Immediately what had been said about Nebuchadnezzar was fulfilled..." (Daniel 4:29-33).

Nebuchadnezzar was under the mistaken assumption that he was responsible for Babylon's prosperity when, in fact, it was God responding to the captive's prayers. Imagine your prison being prospered like Babylon! New dorms, classrooms, and chapels could be built. The chow hall could provide more nutritious and better-tasting food. The facility would offer better jobs with better pay! Education would give higher-level programming. Medical needs could be met immediately and with accuracy. Recreation could get new equipment.

Just think, those are only the material blessings. If you prayed, your prison would be prospered **spiritually** as well! Let me show you what happened to King Nebuchadnezzar after he was driven from his throne. Seven years after he claimed responsibility for Babylon's increase, he experienced a spiritual awakening.

"At the end of that time, I, Nebuchadnezzar, raised my eyes toward heaven, and my sanity was restored. Then I praised the Most High; I honored and glorified Him who lives forever... At the same time that my sanity was restored, my honor and splendor were returned to me for the glory of my kingdom. My advisers and nobles sought me out, and I was restored to my throne and became even greater than before. Now I, Nebuchadnezzar, praise and exalt and glorify the King of heaven, because everything He does is right and all His ways are just..." (Daniel 4:34, 36-37).

Nebuchadnezzar's spiritual conversion left him praising, honoring and glorifying God. Can you imagine what would happen if the officials in your prison experienced the same thing? The entire system would change!

This is not just a far-fetched dream, but also a very real possibility. Think about it. If the prayers of the Israelite captives could change one of the most ruthless kings of the ancient world, your prayers can do the same for the officials in your facility!

Now, what about the prosperity of the prisoners who were doing the praying? Let's take a closer look at the promise given to them.

"Also, seek the peace and prosperity of the city to which I have carried you into exile. ***Pray to the LORD for it, because if it prospers, you too will prosper"*** (Jeremiah 29:7).

The Bible says that if you pray for your place of exile, you will be prospered. Not only in the here and now, but also toward your future because, like the other instructions in Jeremiah's letter, this one is connected to your Expected End. Look at it again. *"Also, seek the peace and prosperity of the city to which I have carried you into exile. Pray to the Lord for it, because if it prospers, you too will prosper."*

"For I know the thoughts that I think toward you, saith the Lord, thoughts of peace, and not of evil, to give you an Expected End" (Jeremiah 29: 11 KJV).

When you pray, God will prosper you by enabling you to be equipped for your Expected End. Let's look at some examples of how Daniel and his fellow captives prospered toward their assignments because they prayed for their place of exile.

Prospering in Wisdom

Wisdom – you need it to navigate throughout your day, and to be successful in your Expected End. God gives two kinds of wisdom: *practical wisdom*, to assist you in daily matters and *spiritual wisdom*, to help you with matters of the spirit. Daniel and his fellow captives were praying for their prison, so therefore God prospered them in both kinds. The Bible says,

"To these four young men God gave knowledge and understanding of all kinds of literature and learning. And Daniel could understand visions and dreams of all kinds" (Daniel 1:17).

First, let's talk about practical wisdom. It is the kind of knowledge God gives you on everything from literature to everyday issues. Having God's practical wisdom will enable you to make right decisions, to have perfect timing and to succeed where others fail. In fact, when God prospers you with practical wisdom; you get a big advantage over the rest of the world. Scripture says the wisdom God gave to Daniel and his fellow captives made them ten times smarter than all the wise men in Babylon!

"In every matter of wisdom and understanding about which the king questioned them, he found them ten times better than all the magicians and enchanters in his whole kingdom" (Daniel 1:20).

When you pray for your facility, God will prosper you in increased practical wisdom, which will put you heads above the world's competition. **This same practical wisdom will also enable you to complete your Expected End!** Let me give you an example from my own life.

I was a computer illiterate who barely knew how to type. For years I wrote *The Captivity Series* by hand then sent it through the mail to my friend, Teresa, who typed it for me. One day, Teresa could no longer work on the manuscript. This situation could have stopped my mission dead in its tracks. Thankfully though, God covered it. A few weeks before this happened, I awoke one morning with a distinct feeling the Lord gave me some kind of supernatural wisdom increase during the night. That very afternoon I sat down and began to type out the book by myself! What happened? God prospered me in practical wisdom to enable me to complete the job He assigned me to do!

Now, what about wisdom concerning the things of the Spirit? The Scripture says, "...and *Daniel could understand visions and dreams of all kinds."* Possessing the ability to understand things of the Spirit is crucial. When you have spiritual wisdom you aren't limited to the natural realm, but have access to supernatural information! The kind of information you will need to be placed into and be successful on your Expected End journey.

If you read the Scriptures, every time Daniel was promoted toward his Expected End, it was because of the supernatural wisdom he possessed. The first time it happened, Daniel interpreted the dream of King Nebuchadnezzar. The Bible says the result of Daniel's spiritual wisdom was,

"Then the king made Daniel great and gave him many great gifts, and he made him to rule over the whole province of Babylon and to be chief governor over all the wise men of Babylon" (Daniel 2:48 AMP).

Daniel's second promotion came when King Belshazzar was feasting with a thousand of his lords. During the banquet, a hand appeared from the supernatural realm to write a message on the wall. Shaken, Belshazzar called for his wise men to interpret the message, but none could. However, when Daniel was summoned, he was able to give an accurate interpretation because of the spiritual wisdom he possessed. The Scripture says, *"...Daniel was clothed with purple and a chain of gold put around his neck, and a proclamation was made concerning him that he should be the third ruler in the kingdom"* (Daniel 5:29 AMP).

Daniel was promoted again! In fact, during his time of imprisonment, Daniel was repeatedly promoted toward his Expected End because of the spiritual wisdom he possessed. Where did Daniel get all this wisdom? Scripture proves he read and obeyed Jeremiah's instructions to pray for Babylon. In return, God fulfilled His promise to prosper him.

Joseph is another example of how God can use spiritual wisdom in promoting you to your Expected End. Joseph spent years training in prison for his assignment, and God used spiritual wisdom to open the door for his promotion. Joseph could interpret dreams and because he accurately interpreted the dreams of Pharaoh, he was placed as second-in-command over all of Egypt!

Over and over again, we read in Scripture how spiritual wisdom played an important role in placing a prisoner in their assignment. When you pray for your facility, God will prosper you with spiritual wisdom, which will enable you to be placed in your Expected End.

Prospering in Favor

Do you remember what the word *favor* means? It means "to make an exception to the rules." Have you ever needed a phone call from your counselor, immediate medical attention, a correspondence clearance, or even a bed move? As you know, these seemingly simple things can be very difficult in prison, unless of course you have favor with an official. **Did you know that six times in Scripture where favor is mentioned, it is in direct reference to an official giving it to an inmate?** Look at Joseph. "...But *while Joseph was there in the prison, the LORD was with him; he showed him kindness and **granted him favor in the eyes of the prison warden**"* (Genesis 39:20-21).

The Bible also talks about Daniel receiving favor from an official in Babylon. *"Now God had **caused the official to show favor** and sympathy to Daniel"* (Daniel 1:9).

Esther received favor from the king when she was a captive in his harem. *"Now the king was attracted to Esther more than to any of the other women, and **she won his favor** and approval..."* (Esther 2:17).

Ezra, the scribe, also received favor from his officials in Babylon. *"this Ezra came up from Babylon... Praise be to the LORD, the God of our fathers... **who has extended his good favor to me before the king and his advisers and all the king's powerful officials...**"* (Ezra 7:6, 27-28).

Nehemiah, while in captivity, received favor from the king. *"...'If it pleases the king and **if your servant has found favor in his sight**, let him send me to the city in Judah* *where my fathers are buried so that I can rebuild it' ...It pleased the king to send me..."* (Nehemiah 2:5-6).

All of these prisoners except Joseph were products of the Babylonian exile. All read Jeremiah's letter and were praying for their place of captivity, which is why they were prospered with favor!

Now, I want you to look again at the above Scriptures so I can show you something very important. In each instance when those prisoners received favor, it was in direct connection to their Expected End!

For Joseph, the warden showed him favor by putting him in charge of the prison. This favor enabled Joseph to receive the training he needed to be qualified for his Expected End!

While Daniel was training to enter into the king's service, God caused his prison official to show him favor. This favor enabled Daniel to climb to his Expected End as head over Babylon. He also became the main prophet in the Bible who foretold of the coming of Christ in the end times!

For Esther, the favor shown her before the king paved the way for her Expected End. She became queen and saved the lives of all the Jews who still remained in the land of captivity!

Ezra spent his time in captivity studying the Scriptures. He received favor from the king that enabled him to go on his mission home to restore service to the temple in Jerusalem and teach the returned exiles the Word of God!

Nehemiah received the favor he needed to pursue his assignment, to rebuild the broken-down walls of Jerusalem! When it came to completing their assignments, all these prisoners received favor! They were prospered with this favor because they were praying for their place of exile. If you obey the instructions in Jeremiah's letter, God will do the same thing for you. He will give you the favor you need to complete your Expected End.

When I was still in county jail, I was trying to get permission to teach Bible studies to all the units in my block. I was repeatedly denied until the facility hired a new pastor. Within a week, I was asked by him and his wife to lead the study even though they didn't know me! You see, I was praying for my place of exile so God gave me favor with those people. In turn, this favor enabled me to get further training for my Expected End!

Prospering in Persecution

Chapter 6 of the book of Daniel is the story of his persecution and being thrown into the lions' den. At that time, Daniel was steadily prospering in his position within Babylon, which unfortunately aroused a lot of jealousy from the other ruling officials in the kingdom. To make matters worse, King Darius planned to make Daniel ruler over the entire realm. When the other officials heard this, they plotted to stop the promotion.

Knowing Daniel was a faithful man of prayer, the officials tricked King Darius into issuing a decree that no one could pray to any god except the king for 30 days. If anyone broke the law, one would be thrown into the lions' den. When Daniel heard the decree, he did not waiver in his commitment to pray. Instead, he went home and, in front of an open window for all to see, *"...he got down on his knees and prayed, giving thanks to his God, just as he had done before"* (Daniel 6:10).

When the officials saw Daniel praying, they hurried to tell the king that Daniel broke the law. When the king heard this, he was very distressed because he knew his proclamation could not be repealed and so Daniel had to be thrown to the lions.

So, the king gave the order. They threw Daniel into the lions' den, and then a rock was placed over the entrance to seal him in. All night, King Darius refused to eat or be entertained, but rather laid awake until morning when he hastened to the den to check on Daniel.

When the king arrived, he called out to Daniel and, sure enough, he was still alive! In fact, Scripture says when Daniel was lifted out of the den, *"...no wound was found on him..."* (Daniel 6:23). How did Daniel survive? He was praying for his prison so God protected His life!

I remember a situation I dealt with when I was in prison. I was working in the kitchen as the head of the floor crew. One day a new girl, who just arrived from state, hit me up for a job. Trying to help her out, I persuaded my supervisor to put her on the crew; but soon afterwards I realized I made a big mistake.

She immediately started making a play for my position. She even attacked my Christianity and made false statements about me in order to get me discredited. Finally, she succeeded in turning one of my supervisors against me, who then made my life at work a living hell! There were times when I wanted to revert back to my old self and just throw down with her, but I knew God would not honor that. So, I continued to pray and believe that God would prosper me through the persecution.

Just when it seemed it couldn't get any worse, I was offered a way-better job doing the floors in visiting! Then, as my enemy watched on, I was asked to do all kinds of side jobs, which paid bonuses like bingo bags full of goodies. Finally, the warden's office made a personal request for me to do their floors! I was told my persecutor was very unhappy about this.

But what does prospering through persecution have to do with your Expected End? Look again at what happened to Daniel. In the beginning of the story, he was about to be promoted to ruler over the entire realm of Babylon. *"Now Daniel so distinguished himself among the administrators and the satraps by his exceptional qualities that the king planned to set him over the whole kingdom"* (Daniel 6:3).

Daniel was about to be put in his highest position ever and his enemies attacked him for it. Satan is your enemy. He is very aware that God is working out a plan to promote you to your Expected End. Thus, he will stop at nothing to prevent it from happening. Why? **Because there is no greater weapon against the kingdom of darkness than a person who is pursuing their created purpose!**

When you take possession of your Expected End, you are like a polished arrow in God's hands, ready and in the right position to completely strike down the enemy! Satan wants to *"kill, steal and destroy"* you, your dreams, and your future hope (John 10:10). His goal is to stop all Christians from attaining their Expected End. You see, as long as we don't take possession of our assignments, we can't hurt him. Satan used those men to attack Daniel because he wanted Daniel stopped before he could destroy the kingdom of darkness. Fortunately, the enemy did not succeed. Daniel became one of the foremost prophets who foretold of satan's downfall and of the coming of Christ in the end times!

There is one last thing I want to point out concerning the persecution Daniel went through. What was Daniel doing when he was attacked? He was praying! When you decide to obey Jeremiah's instructions to pray for your facility, you will face adversity for it. Remember that prayer prospers you toward your Expected End, which means prayer is lethal to the enemy. Satan was so determined to stop Daniel from possessing his assignment; he made Daniel's enemies issue a law against prayer! I love how Daniel responded. Even though he knew his life was in danger, he prayed anyway because he realized the real danger would come if he did not.

Do as Daniel did - Pray! The Bible says *"...Daniel prospered during the reign of Darius and the reign of Cyrus the Persian"* (*Daniel* 6:28). If you follow Daniel's example, you too will be prospered in your Expected End.

Lesson Fourteen

1. The instructions in Jeremiah's letter are intended as preparation for your Expected End. The third instruction: *"Also, seek the peace and prosperity of the city to which I have carried you into exile. Pray to the LORD for it, because if it prospers, you too will prosper"* (Jeremiah 29:7). *"For I know the thoughts that I think toward you, saith the Lord, thoughts of peace and not of evil, to give you an Expected End"* (Jeremiah 29:11 KJV). According to these Scriptures, God wants you to _____ for your place of exile because if it prospers, _____ will prosper too. (Fill in the blanks.)

2. Name some ways that Babylon prospered because of the prisoners' prayers.

3. Name some ways your prison could prosper through your prayers.

4. According to our study, what are three ways you will prosper when you pray for your facility? Remember that each one will aid you in walking out your Expected End.

5. What is one of the most powerful weapons in the universe against the kingdom of darkness? Why?

6. Satan does not want you to take possession of your Expected End. Since prayer prospers you toward your purpose, he will try everything he can to get you to stop. Is there anything right now hindering you from praying? Explain.

CHAPTER FIFTEEN

MY REVELATION

"For if you remain silent at this time, relief and deliverance for the Jews will arise from another place, but you and your father's family will perish. And who knows but that you have come to royal position for such a time as this?"
Esther 4:14

Did you ever wonder what would happen if God spoke to you but you missed what He said? That happened to me at a crucial time in my incarceration: God was giving me revelation of my Expected End but I almost blew it off! The Lord began a miraculous work in my facility when He led four sisters and me to start a ministry inside the prison. By following the instructions in Jeremiah's letter to *"marry and have sons and daughters,"* our little church grew overnight. As a result of our growth, more and more women got involved in the ministry and received the on-the-job training needed to be qualified for their Expected Ends.

I was training in my spot too, teaching Bible studies, and leading worship. However, what I was being prepared for, I didn't know at the time. Although I spent practically every waking minute in service to God through the ministry, something was still missing. What was my future God-job? What were the plans God had in store for me? I loved to teach and I loved music, but I didn't have a clue as to how God would use those gifts for His glory.

Six months after the formation of the ministry, I began teaching a study, which I named *The Captivity Series*. Two-thirds of the way through the *Series*, I began to show my class how to recognize when God was sending them a revelation of their Expected End. To illustrate my point, I used the story of a woman in the Bible named Esther. She was the perfect example for my students because she too was prepared for her assignment through the vehicle of her captivity. However, when the time came for God to reveal to Esther her mission, she almost declined the offer and lost her opportunity.

Esther's narrow escape was the biggest reason why I chose to share her story with my class. The Lord put urgency in my heart that what happened to her was also happening to His people in prison now. They were being prepared for their assignment, but when it came time to receive the revelation of their Expected End, they were missing it.

The Bible study one particular night was packed. God's anointing was present. As I looked out on my class, I saw the women wide-eyed as they listened to the message. I heard "amens" and "hallelujahs" coming from every corner. By the time the night was over, I could see everyone was filled with the anticipation of not only hearing from God, but also responding to the opportunity when it came.

As I watched the ladies hurry out of the classroom with faces lit up, I knew I just gave a sorely needed message. However, little did I realize that, if I should have been preaching to anyone, it was to me, because the next day the Lord started doing exactly what I spoke about - revealing my Expected End. Unfortunately, even though I'd just taught on the importance of not missing the opportunity, I didn't immediately act on mine.

In the days following, the Spirit of the Lord began to place thoughts into my mind of turning *The Captivity Series* into a book. At work, standing in line for chow, just basically at all times, my mind was busy thinking about this "crazy" idea. I say crazy because my insecurities were just as busy telling me it couldn't be done.

First of all, I was not a writer. In fact, most of the time I couldn't even spell correctly. Secondly, I was an inmate, so how was I going to get a book published? Nobody would take me seriously. Thirdly, I realized writing a book was a huge amount of work. Though I didn't want to admit it, maybe I was just too lazy to do it.

Anyway, with all those negative points and more bombarding my mind, I was hoping God didn't actually want me to go through with it. However, my mind, being directed by the Holy Spirit, would not stop dwelling on thoughts about writing down the *Series*. As the days, then weeks went by, I began to feel like I was in the middle of some great tug-of-war contest. Do it! Don't do it! Do it! Don't do it! Back and forth I went. Finally, in order to end the conflict, I tried using my own reasoning to argue with God.

"This can't be from you Lord," I said, being sure I had good reasons to say so. "I'm a speaker, not a writer, and besides," I continued, "there is way too much work involved in writing a book. I wouldn't even know where to start."

Unfortunately, those arguments didn't end the matter, but rather, the wrestling match inside my head raged on, growing in intensity. Then, if this wasn't enough, satan, who understood before I did, that I was on the brink of a discovery that would forever cripple his kingdom, attempted to stop me with his lies.

"What makes you think the revelations you received are special enough to be in a book?" I heard him whisper. As I stood cringing at his belittling words, fear crept in. Then he saw an opportunity to jab at me again.

"Who do you think you are?" he said challengingly. Then giving me no time to recover, he repeated, "You are nothing!" over and over into my mind.

Filled with feelings of insecurity, plus beat up from the struggle, I finally broke and agreed with the deceiver. "I can't do this," I thought; "It would be way too hard for me."

With this as my excuse, I totally dropped the idea and went on my merry way. Or at least I thought I did.

Unfortunately, my way was not merry anymore. I threw myself back into what I always did: teaching, studying, worshiping, and praying, but there was no joy in it like before. Suddenly, I felt like I was constantly bugged, but didn't know why. I was doing the things that had always brought me peace, but instead, I was impatient and unsettled, even offensive to my friends. I felt terrible.

"What's wrong with me, Lord?" I would cry, but He would only answer me by putting more thoughts in my head about writing the book.

Finally, I couldn't take the struggle anymore, so I relented. I decided to talk to another Christian sister about a book she'd been working on. Sister Dana was writing a story about her life. Feeling like she could shed some light on my dilemma, I headed toward the recreation field to seek her out. As I walked through the compound, I began to talk silently with my Lord.

"If you want me to do this Father," I said in my mind, "give me clear confirmation through Dana."

When I entered into the recreation barn, I saw Dana was just finishing her workout and was packing her gym bag. So, I quickly walked up to her, said my greetings, and then got right to the point.

"I don't want to seem like a copycat, but I think the Lord might be telling me to turn *The Captivity Series* into a book."

When I said it, she instantly stopped what she was doing to stare at me with a look of astonishment. Then gesturing broadly with her arms, she blurted out, "I can't believe you said that!" My heart barely skipped a beat before she continued, "God has been putting it on my heart to talk to you about writing down the *Series*!"

The confirmation I'd just prayed for was instant! It left me somewhat stunned, but Dana didn't seem to notice my demeanor because she just kept going on, appearing to be under the control of the Holy Spirit.

"The Bible studies on the captivities are incredible," she continued with much enthusiasm. "I've never heard a teaching like it before!" At this, the Lord replayed in my mind the exact opposite words I'd heard from satan just days before. Indeed, I was lied to, but this realization didn't stop my fears from rising again.

"But I'm not a writer, I am a speaker!" I protested to her. "So I wouldn't even know where to begin."

"Just write it like you would teach it in class," Dana responded with the confidence I didn't have. "Start by making an outline for the whole book," she began, raising one finger as though counting out steps. "Then choose how many pages your chapters will be and stay within your page range," she added, raising a second finger. "Then all you have to do from there is start writing from your outline!" At this, her third finger popped out, and then she broadly gestured with both hands as to emphasize her last point.

However, Dana wasn't anywhere close to being done. In fact, she was just getting warmed up. Realizing the yard would be closed soon, she continued talking while grabbing the rest of her things. Then pausing only to take a breath and slip on her eyeglasses, she started up again while turning to leave the building.

As we continued to walk and talk, Dana systematically thrust through my remaining insecurities with bold statements on the power and importance of *The Captivity Series.* As I watched her flay her hands about, I couldn't help but think that, with her glasses on, she looked like a possessed schoolteacher. However, as I continued to listen to her, I realized I was gaining courage with her every word. The more she talked, the more I knew I needed to get off my butt and get started.

Finally, we reached the place in the compound where we parted company. This is when Dana suddenly turned to me to wrap-up her speech with a very sobering statement, "If you decide you're not going to do it, Katie, I would like to write it for you."

When I heard her say it, I realized that, although God put me in as lead quarterback for this game, there were other players eagerly waiting on the bench in case my arm gave out. This meant that, if I didn't take Him up on His offer soon, I could very well lose my opportunity. This project was going to get done whether I chose to be involved or not.

That night in my cell, the Lord began to fill my head with ideas of how to begin. In fact, He started pouring in so much information I couldn't sleep. Finally, I decided to resign myself to His overwhelming Presence, and scaring my cellmates, I bolted upright in my bed and said aloud,

"All right, already Lord, please slow down!" Then reaching for a paper and pen, I began to take notes. The next day after work I went back to my cell to get started. After a few hours of writing, I stopped to reread what I wrote. "Not bad!" I said, talking to myself.

Then I got up to go to one of my prayer meetings and, out of nowhere, I suddenly burst into tears. Holding on to the edge of the sink for support, I wept uncontrollably. In fact, the ensuing torrent was so strong I put a piece of paper up in the window of my cell so people, who were now curiously looking in, couldn't see.

When my tears finally subsided, I wondered where they came from. However, strangely enough, even though I just sobbed my eyes out, I was filled with a feeling of total gratefulness to God! I didn't understand it then, but shortly afterward, the Lord showed me the answer. My unusual response came from my obedience to take action on the revelation of my Expected End.

From that day forward, I was filled with a supernatural kind of joy! Unlike ordinary happiness, which lasts for a moment, I experienced an intense feeling of excitement and satisfaction bubbling up inside of me for the months and even years to come. As I continued to work on the book, I began to realize I was receiving this heavenly joy because I was pursuing my Expected End: the very purpose for which I was created!

Today, whenever I look back at how I struggled with my revelation, I am grateful for the Bible study that started it all. Knowing Esther almost passed up her assignment gives me hope. Unfortunately, there are untold thousands of prisoners in captivity right now who are in danger of missing the revelation of their future. Because I experienced such a close call, I know how easily it can happen. This is why the most important factor of my assignment now is to make sure you don't miss yours.

Lesson Fifteen

1. Describe, in detail, your current activities in the body of Christ.

2. Have any thoughts or ideas been repeatedly coming to your mind? Describe them.

3. Have you taken action on those thoughts or are you ignoring them? If you've been ignoring them, write down the reasons why.

4. How have you been feeling lately? Use words like happy, depressed, energetic, or confused.

5. Now reread your list of feelings and directly associate them with whether or not you have been taking action on the thoughts repeatedly placed in your mind. *Example: I haven't taken action on those thoughts and I've been feeling agitated.*

CHAPTER SIXTEEN

GET IT BEFORE YOU GO

"Now there was in the citadel of Susa a Jew of the tribe of Benjamin, named Mordecai son of Jair, the son of Shimei, the son of Kish, who had been carried into exile from Jerusalem by Nebuchadnezzar king of Babylon... Mordecai had a cousin Hadassah... also known as Esther..."
Esther 2:5-7

The above genealogy is found in the book of Esther. It traces the descendants of a man named Kish, one of the first prisoners taken to Babylon, to a man named Mordecai and his cousin, Esther. These two people, descendants of the original Babylonian captives, will be our focus for the next few chapters. From their example, I am going to show you how to recognize, and then act on, the revelation of your Expected End.

Their story takes place in Susa after the Persians conquered Babylon. At this time, though thousands of Jews were freed to go home to Jerusalem, many more stayed behind in the land of captivity. The book of Esther details the true historical account of how God, through Esther and Mordecai, prevented the total annihilation of those people.

This heroic event took place around 486 B.C. in Susa, the capital of the Persian Empire. The king who was in power at that time was a man named Ahasuerus. After having a fall out with his wife, Queen Vashti, Ahasuerus removed her from the throne, and began a search for a beautiful young virgin to replace her. The king appointed officers in all the provinces of Persia to gather up qualified young maidens, to be brought into his harem.

Now, Mordecai's cousin, Esther, was very beautiful so she was taken into the custody of the king. Mordecai, fearing for her safety, warned her not to speak to anyone of her Jewish heritage. He was so concerned about her that he spent his days walking before the court of the harem to learn what would become of his cousin.

Inside the palace Esther was put under the care of Hegai, the keeper of the king's harem. Immediately, Esther won Hegai's favor. He provided her with seven of the palace's own maids, and then moved her to the best part of the harem. For the next 12 months, Esther, and all the other virgins, received the prescribed beauty treatments that were needed for their night with King Ahasuerus. When the time arrived, each girl was sent individually to the king, bearing a gift of her own choosing. After spending the night, she would be returned to the harem. None of the maidens would come to Ahasuerus again unless he was so delighted with her that he called her by name.

When it came time for Esther to go see the king, she chose to take with her only that which Hegai, the king's eunuch, suggested. Now, Ahasuerus was attracted more to Esther than any other woman. Because she won his favor, the king chose to set a royal crown on her head, making her his queen.

In the king's court was an Agagite, named Haman, whom the king set high above all the other royal officials. Each day Haman would pass through the king's gate and all the people would bow and pay reverence to him. Everyone, that is except Mordecai, who refused to do so. That continued day after day, enraging Haman. Then when he found out Mordecai was a Jew, he sought to destroy not only Mordecai, but the other Jews as well.

Driven to see his plan through, Haman went before Ahasuerus and falsely claimed that the Israelites, who were scattered throughout the kingdom, were not obeying the king's laws so they should be totally annihilated. The king, still unaware of Esther's heritage, agreed with Haman, giving him permission to do as he pleased. So, an edict was issued in Ahasuerus's name for every Israelite throughout the kingdom to be destroyed and their belongings seized as spoil. Copies of the edict were sent out to every province. Then, a great mourning began among the exiles. When Mordecai found out, he tore his clothes, put on sackcloth and ashes, and stood crying before the king's gate.

Meanwhile, inside the palace, Queen Esther was totally unaware of the deadly decree. When she heard of Mordecai's behavior at the gate, she sent one of her maids to find out what was wrong. However, Mordecai refused to speak to her, so the queen sent one of the king's eunuchs instead. This time, Mordecai explained what happened. He gave the eunuch a copy of the decree to take back to Esther, along with a message urging her to appear before King Ahasuerus to beg for her peoples' lives.

When Esther heard what Mordecai asked her to do, she became very afraid. You see, in Persia there was a law stating that no one could see the king unless he or she was first summoned. Whoever broke this law would be put to death, unless the king showed them grace by extending his golden scepter. To make matters worse, it appeared as if the king didn't want to see Esther because he had not called for her in a month. Fearing for her life, Esther sent a message back to Mordecai saying she didn't want to do as he asked. When Mordecai received her answer, his return reply was severe. He said,

"...Do not think that because you are in the king's house you alone of all the Jews will escape. For if you remain silent at this time, relief and deliverance for the Jews will arise from another place, but you and your father's family will perish. And who knows but that you have come to royal position for such a time as this?" (Esther 4:13-14).

Esther faced the decision of a lifetime. Should she remain silent and possibly perish or risk death by going before the king? Was she, as Mordecai said, placed in her royal position as queen for such a time as this?

Based on Mordecai's response, Esther decided to take action. She sent a message back instructing him to gather the Jews and have them fast for three days while she and her maids did the same. At the end of the message she wrote, "...*When this is done, I will go to the king, even though it is against the law. And if I perish, I perish*" (Esther 4:16).

Three days later, the fast was over and the hour arrived. Esther put on her royal robes. She then walked into the king's inner court, even though she was not summoned. As Ahasuerus looked upon his queen, she obtained favor in his sight. He extended to her his golden scepter, and then announced he would grant her whatever she might ask, even up to half his kingdom. So, Esther requested that the king attend a banquet she would prepare, and to bring Haman as his guest. The king accepted and Haman was summoned at once so they could do as Esther bid.

The night of the feast, the king again asked Esther what her petition was but she wisely remained silent. Instead, she chose to further cultivate the king's favor by asking him to attend a second banquet, which is when she would expose Haman's plot. So, the first feast ended with no one aware of Esther's true intentions.

That night, as Haman headed home through the city gate, he saw Mordecai refuse to bow to him. Enraged, Haman went and told his family. They suggested Haman build a gallows 75 feet high, on which to hang Mordecai. The idea so delighted Haman, he immediately ordered it to be done.

Meanwhile, in the palace, the king was having a hard time sleeping so he ordered his attendant to read to him the book of the Chronicles. When the attendant started going through the various events, which took place in the kingdom, he came across a story about Mordecai exposing a plot to assassinate the king. When Ahasuerus asked his attendant what honor and recognition Mordecai received for his deed, the answer was none.

At this moment, Haman entered the court to talk to the king about hanging Mordecai on the gallows! However, before Haman could speak, Ahasuerus asked him what he thought should be done for the man the king wished to honor. Haman, believing the king wanted to honor him, told Ahasuerus the man should be dressed in a royal robe then mounted on a horse and led around by one of the king's most noble princes, who should proclaim, "This is what is done for the man the king delights to honor!" Upon hearing this advice, the king ordered Haman to go at once to do as he suggested for Mordecai, the Jew!

So, Haman got the robe and horse, robed Mordecai, then led him through the streets proclaiming to all that he was honored by the king. Afterward, Haman was so humiliated he rushed home to tell his wife, but barely got the story out before the king's eunuchs arrived to hurry him away to Esther's banquet.

During the second feast, the king again asked Esther to tell him her petition. Reassuring her that, whatever it was, it would be given to her, even up to half the kingdom. It was then Esther chose to act. She began her request by pleading with the king to spare her life, along with the lives of her people, because both had been sold into total annihilation. When the king asked Esther who dared do such a thing, she answered by saying the adversary and enemy was the vile Haman! Enraged, the king left his wine and went out to the palace gardens.

Haman was totally terrified! Realizing Ahasuerus already decided his fate, he stayed behind in the palace to beg the queen for his life. Just as he fell on the couch where Esther was reclined, the king returned and in a further rage accused Haman of trying to molest the queen. As those words left the king's mouth, the palace eunuchs grabbed Haman. He was to be hanged on the very gallows he built for Mordecai.

That day, the king called Mordecai into his presence, and then Esther was given Haman's vast estate. Unfortunately, even though Haman's plot was uncovered, time was still running out for the Jews. The order for their annihilation was only months away from being executed. So, Esther pleaded with the king to allow a second order to be issued to override the first. Ahasuerus responded by commanding a decree be written giving the Israelites permission to protect themselves and their property. So, Mordecai summoned the royal secretaries and had this new decree sent out by couriers on royal horses to the 127 provinces stretching from India to Cush.

On the thirteenth day of the twelfth month, the month of Adar, the new edict was executed. On that day, the enemies of the Jews who hoped to overpower Israel had the tables turned on them. The Jews gathered together with no one able to oppose them! They slew over 75,000 of their opponents. The fear of the Jews became so great many people chose to become Jews themselves. It was a joyous time, which became known as the Jewish holiday, Purim.

The lives of untold numbers of Israelites living in the land of captivity were saved because one woman chose to act on the revelation of her Expected End! Esther, however, almost rejected her opportunity when it was first presented to her.

What almost happened to Esther is exactly what is happening to a vast number of prisoners today. They are failing to act when the revelation of their assignment arrives. Few people ever get to experience the fullness of the future God has for them because they just plain miss it! In this chapter and the next, we are going to discuss how to prevent this from happening to you. Before we start, I want to clarify a few quick points concerning the importance of receiving the revelation of your Expected End.

God's Plan vs. your plan

"Many plans are in a man's mind, but it is the Lord's purpose for him that will stand" (Proverbs 19:21 AMP).

Human beings are natural planners. We like to think and talk about all the things we are planning to do. However, the Bible says all our planning is useless because only God's purposes for our lives will stand. This is why you must find out what God's purposes are for you specifically.

Only your Creator knows what you were created to be. You cannot possibly know what it is unless He tells you! Author Rick Warren talks about this in his famed book, *"The Purpose Driven Life."*

"If I handed you an invention you had never seen before, you wouldn't know its purpose, and the invention itself wouldn't be able to tell you either. Only the creator or the owner's manual could reveal its purpose."

God is your Creator, so only He knows exactly what you were created to be. This is why you must consult Him to find out your Expected End. Unfortunately, many people never bother to ask the Father about their future. Instead, they just come up with their own bright ideas. However, the Bible says when you choose to pursue your own plans and not God's, you will fail.

"The LORD foils the plans of the nations; he thwarts the purposes of the peoples. But the plans of the LORD stand firm forever, the purposes of his heart through all generations" (Psalm 33:10-11).

This Scripture makes it plain: If you choose to pursue your own plans instead of God's, He will actually prevent you from succeeding in whatever you do! Why would God cause you to fail? Not to punish you, but rather to get you to give up on your own powerless ideas to join Him in His eternal work.

You see, God's plans are perfect. They have far-reaching Kingdom purposes. One assignment from Him can leave more impact on the world than a million of your own "good" ideas. In the next chapter, I am going to tell you how to recognize when God is revealing His plan to you.

Knowledge of your Expected End will change the way you do the rest of your time

Nothing is worse than doing prison time, day after day, year after year, without joy. Have you ever had a day when you woke up in your cell thinking you just couldn't take it any longer? God does not want you to feel this way! He wants you to be able to do your time with joy! Possessing the knowledge of your Expected End will give you this joy.

Let me prove it to you. Look again at what God said to the Babylonian captives in Jeremiah's letter: *"For I know the plans I have for you...* **plans to give you hope...** *an Expected End."*

One of the reasons why God reveals your Expected End is to give you hope. Biblical hope is not some wishy-washy daydream, but rather a certainty of things yet to come. Having possession of your assignment means you have a hopeful and **guaranteed** future. This guarantee will give you hope. If you are filled with hope, you will have the ability to cope, no matter what your situation.

Scripture says, *"...the joy of the LORD is your strength"* (Nehemiah 8:10). Hope gives you joy. Joy will give you the strength to endure. Do you know how Jesus endured the extreme pain of the cross? Through the joy He received from knowing His Expected End; to be the Savior and Redeemer of the whole world! Hebrews 12:2 says, *"Let us fix our eyes on Jesus, the author and perfecter of our faith, who for the joy set before him endured the cross..."*

The joy Jesus received from knowing what His mission on earth would accomplish enabled Him to endure being whipped, beaten and even crucified! Joy will enable you to endure the cross of your imprisonment. The knowledge of your Expected End will bring you this joy.

Countless prisoners, even Christians, are in a hopeless existence. They have no joy and nothing to look forward to because they do not know what their future holds. As soon as I received the revelation of my Expected End, the months seemed to fly by! I was filled with so much excitement at the thought of my future; there were days when it didn't even seem like I was in prison! When you finally act on the revelation of your future hope, the rest of your days inside will be filled with purpose. This purpose will change the way you do your time.

God wants to reveal your Expected End while you are on the inside, so you can make it on the outside

Do you remember, in Solomon's prayer, God's third purpose for your time?

"And if they turn back to you with all their heart and soul in the land of their enemies who took them captive... *then... hear their prayer and their plea, and uphold their cause"* (1 Kings 8:48-49).

The way you fulfill God's third purpose is by totally surrendering to His will for your life **while** you are in the land of captivity. **This means taking possession of your**

Expected End while you are still incarcerated! Why is it so important for you to get a revelation of your future on the inside of the wire?

The recidivism rate for ex-felons is about 70%. This means seven out of 10 people who get out of prison go back! Why are the numbers so high? **Because when people get out, they pursue their own plans instead of God's, so they fail!** Remember what the Bible says, if you are not pursuing the purposes God has planned for your life, you won't succeed in anything you do. Even if you are doing a "good" thing! What happens when a person gets out and all the plans they make fail? They go back to what they know in order to survive, which usually means drugs, crime, and then a return to prison.

Do you remember the warning Jeremiah gave the Israelites? He said the chastisement of their captivity would continue until it accomplished its purpose. (Jeremiah 4:22 AMP). The chastisement of your captivity will continue if you don't have God's plan when you get out! Without His plan you will fail and go back to prison! God wants you to remain free and live an abundant life. The best way to ensure this is to grab hold of His plans for your future **now** while you are still here.

God wants to give you your assignment while you are on the inside. Let me show you proof. Take another look at Jeremiah's letter to the exiles. Notice the **order** in which it was written.

The **first** thing listed in the letter is the instructions to prepare you for your Expected End.

"Build...and ...plant...increase in number...pray..."

The **second** thing listed is the promise of your Expected End.

"For I know the thoughts that I think toward you... to give you an Expected End."

The **third,** and last thing, is the promise that the captives will go home.

"I... will bring you back to the place from which I carried you into exile."

Now look at the order carefully. The revelation of the Expected End comes **before** the release to go home! This proves God wants to give you your revelation before you get out! I love the way the King James Version of Jeremiah 29:11 reads. It says God knows the thoughts of the future He thinks *"toward you."* This means that, while you are here, God will send the details of His plans from His Spirit **"toward"** your mind so you can receive the knowledge of your Expected End (1 Corinthians 2:9-16).

Every major captive in the Bible received a revelation about their Expected End while they were in captivity. Joseph, Daniel, Esther, Zerubbabel, Jeshua, Ezra, and Nehemiah were all given their assignments while they were still inside. Each one of them, whether they stayed in exile or were released to go home, completed their assignment and tasted the fullness of the life God planned for them.

God wants all His captive people to receive the revelation of their Expected End while they are on the inside so they will be armed with His indestructible plan when they get out! I received my assignment to write this study while I was still in prison. In fact, I wrote over half this book from behind the walls. Once I was released, I experienced the power that possessing my Expected End gave to me. It enabled me to fight off temptation and to stay out of prison. It empowered me to succeed where I would have otherwise failed. It filled me with joy and caused me to live an abundant, purpose-filled life!

It is very important for you to discover and act upon the revelation of your Expected End while you are in captivity. In the next chapter we are going to explore why most prisoners miss their revelation. You are also going to learn how to prevent this from happening to you.

Lesson Sixteen

1. Do you see any of yourself or your situation in Esther's story? If so, in what ways?

2. What does the following verse mean to you? *"The LORD foils the plans of the nations; he thwarts the purposes of the peoples. But the plans of the LORD stand firm forever, the purposes of his heart through all generations"* (Psalm 33:10-11).

3. According to the above verse, if you pursue your own plans instead of the Lord's, you will fail. So, whose plan will bring you total success? Yours or God's? Why?

4. Having the knowledge of your Expected End while you are on the inside will change the way you do the rest of your time. Having possession of your assignment means you have a **guaranteed** future to look forward to and this guarantee will give you hope. If you are filled with hope, you will have the ability to cope no matter what your situation. Jeremiah 29:11 says, *"For I know the plans I have for you... plans **to give you hope**... an Expected End."* Rewrite this verse in the space below and underline the words *"to give you hope."*

5. God wants to reveal your Expected End while you are on the inside so you will be able to make it when you get out. Do you remember God's third purpose for your time mentioned in Solomon's prayer? *"And if they turn back to you with all their heart and soul **in the land of their enemies who took them captive**... then... hear their prayer and their plea, and uphold their cause"* (1 Kings 8:48-49). According to this verse, **where** does God want you to take possession of your Expected End?

CHAPTER SEVENTEEN

Why You Miss It

"...and who knows but that you have come to royal position for such a time as this?"
Esther 4:14

"*For such a time as this*" is a dream missed by so many. Why is the promise of an Expected End so elusive? There should be an army of prisoners on the inside and a mass of ex-felons on the outside, taking territory for the Kingdom of God, but there is not. In this chapter we are going to explore some of the many reasons why a large percentage of prisoners miss the revelation of their Expected End.

The reason why I told you the story of Esther and Mordecai in the last chapter was so I could use their example in this chapter to help you recognize and act on your assignment. Now, I am going to teach you the keys to receiving your revelation. So, let's begin.

Do you remember what Mordecai did after He found out about Haman's plot to destroy the Jews? He sent a message to Esther asking her to go before King Ahasuerus to beg for the lives of her people. However, when Esther heard what Mordecai wanted her to do, she became afraid and did not want to go. Well, when Mordecai received her answer, he sent back a second message so profound we are going to use it as our study tool to guide you to your Expected End. Let's review Mordecai's response to Esther again in 4:13-14.

"...Do not think that because you are in the king's house you alone of all the Jews will escape. For if you remain silent at this time, relief and deliverance for the Jews will arise from another place, but you and your father's family will perish. And who knows but that you have come to royal position for such a time as this."

How can you ensure that you don't miss out on the Expected End God has for you? Let's look at each part of Mordecai's answer to discover the powerful ways it can help you get to your created purpose. We will begin with the last part of his statement.

*"And who knows but that you have come to royal **position** for such a time as this?"*

The reason many inmates don't get the revelation of their Expected End is because they are not in the right position to receive it. In Chapter Twelve of this study, we discussed the principle of being involved in the family of God. The reasons God wants you to be involved with the body are two-fold. First, you must be active in the fellowship in order to be trained for your Expected End. Second, **you need to be in your position in the body in order to receive the revelation of your assignment.**

Let me explain. Notice God revealed to Esther her mission **after** she was in her *"royal position"* as queen. What would have happened if Esther were asked to stop the slaughter of the Jews **before** she was queen? Nothing! She wouldn't have known what to do about the problem or possessed any power or ability to change it! As queen, however, Esther knew exactly how the royal court worked. She knew what procedures were required to get to the king. As queen, she also possessed the ability and position to approach the king to ask for her people's lives.

You need to be in *"royal position"* before you can receive your revelation. Only after you have served in your place in the body will you be able to understand and act on your assignment. I was already in my position in the fellowship when the Lord told me to write *The Captivity Series*. In fact, I was teaching this very study when I received my revelation, which is why I understood and could act on what God was telling me to do!

God wants you in your *"royal position"* so you can be ready to receive the knowledge of your Expected End. If you haven't gotten a Divine Revelation about your future, it may be because you're not in your spot in the body. If you feel the Lord is convicting you to join in now, don't hesitate. Get involved and get ready to receive.

The second reason people miss the revelation of their Expected End is because they don't recognize when God is speaking to them. How can you know for sure when you are hearing God's voice and not just your own thoughts?

The way God speaks is through the Holy Spirit. God's Spirit plants His thoughts into your spirit while simultaneously sending the same thought into your mind. In other words, when you receive direction from God, you will just "know" in your gut you are supposed to do something. This knowing will be accompanied by a parallel thought.

Let me give you an example. Say, while you were reading about getting in your royal position, you just somehow "knew" that you were supposed to get involved in the fellowship. If you stop and think about that moment, you will realize you also received a corresponding thought. It may have sounded something like, "I need to join in!"

However, sometimes we are unable to distinguish whether the thought was from God or ourselves. Why? Because many times we get God's direction in the first person, **"I"** form. **"I** need to join in." and also we hear it **in our own voice!** It can almost sound like your own conscience talking to you. So, how do you tell the difference?

When God first started telling me to write down *The Captivity Series*, I got thoughts like, **"I** should write a book" or, **"I** need to get started." Unfortunately, for various reasons, I didn't immediately act on those thoughts. In fact, I finally just blew them off. And when I did, I began to get very uptight. The more time I spent ignoring those thoughts, the more agitated I became. Finally, I reached the point where I was totally miserable, but yet didn't recognize why.

This feeling of agitation was my telltale sign I was hearing from God, but not obeying Him. My lack of peace was my indicator I was missing God's voice. Do you remember what Mordecai said to Esther when she refused to take action on the revelation of her Expected End? He said, *"For if you **remain silent** at this time... **you will perish."*** Once God speaks His plan into your spirit, then you remain silent, not acting on it, your spirit and God's Spirit will begin contending with one another. This raging wrestling match will continue, increasing in intensity, as long as you remain disobedient.

When God speaks, and you fail to act, it will feel as though you are literally **perishing!** This is ultimately why Mordecai told Esther she would perish if she remained silent. He knew she would experience the extreme pain that contending with God in disobedience brings.

Lack of peace means you are out of God's will. This is one sure indicator on how you can discern whether or not God is speaking to you. Are you feeling distressed, confused or uneasy but don't know why? Is there a reoccurring idea in your mind you are ignoring? It is probably an idea from the Father. Since you are remaining silent, you feel as though you are perishing.

If God is speaking and you aren't responding, you could very well be missing out on the revelation of your, *"for such a time as this."* Check your vital signs to see if you are perishing. If so, do not delay, act on the thoughts God is sending. When your perishing feelings change to peace, you will know you are hearing and obeying God.

A third reason a lot of prisoners miss possessing their Expected End is fear. Let's look at how Esther responded to Mordecai when he asked her to go before the king to beg for the lives of her people. She said, *"...any man or woman who approaches the king in the inner court without being summoned the king has but one law: that he be put to death... thirty days have passed since I was called to go to the king"* (Esther 4:11).

Esther's reaction to the revelation of her mission was fear. Fear of death and fear of inadequacy. Esther feared going before the king because she might literally lose her life, but she also felt inadequate because the king hadn't called for her in 30 days.

Fear of death and fear of inadequacy are two things that can cause a person to lose out on their Expected End. Let's take a look at each one of these fears so you can recognize when they are attacking you. First, the fear of death.

When you get a good idea in your mind, your first reaction is to get excited. You begin to think about it all the time. You even go around telling people about it. Then something happens; you realize that, for your idea to become a reality, you must take action - or be like everybody else and just talk about it for the rest of your life!

This is where fear of death comes in to separate the mice from the men, so to speak. Subconsciously, we fear accepting God's assignments because it will mean the death of our own lifestyles, our comfort zones, and our personal agendas. Pursuing God's plan means change and sacrifice. There will be many times when you will have to work on your assignment when you'd rather be doing something else. This is why so many people lose out on their dreams. They don't want to give up their own leisure or take a risk and exert themselves.

As human beings, we naturally reject change by wanting to preserve our comforts and ourselves. Think about Esther. When she heard Mordecai's request, I'm sure at first she had many selfish thoughts. Yes, she didn't want to die, but she probably also didn't want to lose her new position and lifestyle. After all, no one in the palace knew she was Jewish so, if she kept her mouth shut, she could go on living her wonderful life as queen. However, Mordecai was quick to remind her that even if she tried to take the easy way out, she would perish anyway.

This is what people don't understand. When you choose your own life and comfort over God's plan, you will die anyway. Your silence and unwillingness to act will cause you to perish. However, when you choose to get out of your comfort zone, take risks, and give up certain things, your life will be better than you can imagine! Look at Esther. When she finally chose to lay her life on the line to pursue her mission, she was vastly rewarded! She remained queen, experienced the privilege of saving the lives of her people, and also received the gift of Haman's vast estate!

I remember when God told me to quit my job to go into full-time ministry. At first, I hesitated because I didn't want my lifestyle to change. I liked the standard of living my paycheck afforded me. It was nice to have money, to be able to get my hair done and buy new clothes. Eventually though, I realized I needed to die to my own selfish agenda. Now, like Esther, I am experiencing the privilege of saving the lives of people who are in captivity today. Needless to say, this gives me unspeakable joy and fills me with gratitude! In addition to that, God has provided for me, a hundred-fold for the sacrifice I made (Mark 10:29-30).

The second fear that prevents people from taking possession of their Expected End is the fear of inadequacy. Esther felt inadequate because the king didn't call her into his presence for a month. I am sure many fearful thoughts invaded her mind. Did the king no longer desire her or perhaps he thought she wasn't good enough for him? Thoughts of inadequacy can be very powerful. They can emotionally cripple even the most confident person. Look at Esther. The Bible says she was very beautiful, but even so, she still let her fear of inadequacy make her believe the king didn't want her.

Let me give you a warning. The enemy, satan, and your own mind will try to convince you that you are insufficiently equipped to take on God's chosen work. I remember satan telling me I was nobody. He said my revelations weren't important enough to be in a book. Those thoughts, coupled with the fear that I wasn't qualified to write this study, almost prevented me from taking action on my assignment!

I want to show you proof from the Bible that God will never give you an assignment you cannot handle. Let's look in the book of Matthew at the parable of the talents.

*"Again, it will be like a man going on a journey, who called his servants and entrusted his property to them. To one he gave five talents of money, to another two talents, and to another one talent, **each according to his ability.** Then he went on his journey.*

"The man who had received the five talents went at once and put his money to work and gained five more. So also, the one with the two talents gained two more. But the man who had received the one talent went off, dug a hole in the ground and hid his master's money.

"After a long time the master of those servants returned and settled accounts with them. The man who had received the five talents brought the other five. 'Master,' he said, 'you entrusted me with five talents. See, I have gained five more.' His master replied, 'Well done, good and faithful servant! You have been faithful with a few things; I will put you in charge of many things. Come and share your master's happiness!'

"The man with the two talents also came. 'Master,' he said, 'you entrusted me with two talents; see, I have gained two more.' His master replied, 'Well done, good and faithful servant! You have been faithful with a few things; I will put you in charge of many things. Come and share your master's happiness!

*"Then the man who had received the one talent came. 'Master,' he said, 'I knew that you are a hard man, harvesting where you have not sown and gathering where you have not scattered seed. So I was **afraid** and went out and hid your talent in the ground...'"* (Matthew 25:14-25).

In the parable of the talents, the master gave three of His servants' talents to work with while he was gone on a journey. The Scripture says two of those servants took their talents and went to work at once, doubling back their original investment.

However, the third servant did not take action on his talent, but rather hid it in the ground. When the master returned, the servant said he didn't pursue his mission because he was *"afraid."* In reality, there was no reason for him to fear because the master didn't ask him to do more than he could handle. Look at the beginning of the parable. It says the master gave his servants talents, *"**each according to his ability."*** This Scripture proves God will only ask you to do what He has already equipped you to do.

God will supernaturally enable you to complete every mission He sends you on. I remember one night in prison while working on the book, I really began to struggle. I just couldn't seem to get a certain chapter right. As the night wore on, I started to feel so un-anointed, un-able, and un-worthy. In fact, after a few hours, I even began to question whether or not God called me at all.

Finally, in a fit of frustration, I screamed in my mind "Lord, help me!" Immediately, I heard Him say, **"I'm right here."** His voice was so clear at first it startled me; but then, quickly, His words washed away my doubts and fears, then my writing began to flow again. **From then on, I knew that because God gave me this assignment, He would always be with me to make sure it was completed!**

The Father will never send you on a mission you can't finish. Unfortunately, many people let their feelings of inadequacy prevent them from acting on their revelation. What happens when you let fear talk you out of your assignment? The Bible says **you will lose your opportunity!** Let's look again to what Mordecai told Esther in response to her fear.

*"...Do not think that because you are in the king's house you alone of all the Jews will escape. **For if you remain silent at this time, relief and deliverance for the Jews will arise from another place,** but you and your father's family will perish..."*

Mordecai warned Esther that, if she did not take action on her assignment, relief and deliverance for the Jews would come through another source. God had a plan to save His people and His first intention was to use Esther to carry out this plan. However, if Esther chose not to get involved, the mission would still take place with or without her.

The Lord wants to use **you** to accomplish His plans. Unfortunately, if He repeatedly presents His idea without you taking Him up on the offer, He will find someone else who will.

Quickly, go back to the parable of the talents. Look at what the master said to the third servant when, out of fear, he failed to take action on his assignment.

*"You wicked, lazy servant! **Take the talent from him and give it to the one who has the ten talents."***

Because the third servant refused to act on his mission, the master took away his talent then gave it to someone else!

Do you remember my conversation with Sister Dana when I went to talk to her about writing *The Captivity Series*? The last thing she said to me was that, if I didn't want to write the book, she would do it for me. Do you understand what God was doing in her heart? He was preparing her in case I declined my assignment. Don't let fears of inadequacy cause you to pass up your mission! Just remember that God will never give you more than you can handle.

The fourth and biggest reason why people miss out on their Expected End is laziness. Look again at the third servant in the parable of the talents. This man claimed he didn't take action on his assignment because he was *"afraid."* Now, check out the interesting response the master gave to his statement. The master said, *"You **wicked and lazy** servant."* Notice the master didn't call the servant fearful as he claimed he was. Instead, the master chastised him for being lazy! God knows the heart of man better than the man himself does. The servant may have been afraid, but the master knew he was also unwilling to do the work required to complete his assignment!

There is a condition on your future dreams coming to pass. You must do your part! You may think it would be exciting to do a radio or TV ministry, but it actually takes a huge amount of work! You must be disciplined in order to take possession of your future. I didn't just get Expected End Ministries handed to me.

I labored for years in preparation for it. In fact, it took me four years just to write this study, then another year to get it published and get the ministry off the ground! Writing a book and starting a ministry are hard work. Both require a lot of discipline. There were times when I had to overcome the urge to slack off, but, because I chose to be diligent to see my mission to its completion, I am now reaping the rewards.

Many people miss out on their Expected End because they procrastinate on getting started. Or they start full tilt then fade away! You must make a full commitment to your mission, and then carry your commitment to the end, no matter how long it takes. If you don't, your laziness, like fear, could cause you to lose possession of your dream. Look again at what the master said to the servant who was too lazy to work on his assignment.

"You wicked, lazy servant! Take the talent from him and give it to the one who has the ten talents" (Matthew 25:26, 28).

Right now, some of you are procrastinating or have given up working on your assignment. Danger! Beware! Your talent is about to be removed from you and given to someone else. It's not too late! Overcome your weak flesh. Make a decision to set aside time every day to pursue your purpose. **More than anything else, being faithful to work on your assignment is what will enable you to reach your goal and achieve your dreams!**

Another reason why many people miss the revelation of their Expected End is because they reject the thoughts God is putting in their minds. This happens because those thoughts don't make sense to them. Let me explain. When God told me to write this book, it didn't make sense to me because I never considered myself a writer. But let's see what Scripture says about this.

*"Lean on, trust in, and be confident in the Lord with all your heart and mind and **do not rely on your own insight or understanding.** In all your ways know, recognize, and acknowledge Him, and He will direct and make straight and plain your paths"* (Proverbs 3:5-6 AMP).

When it comes to the revelation of your Expected End, you must put aside all your own thoughts and ideas. Any insights you may think you know about your future will only get in the way of receiving the true knowledge of your created purpose.

Also, a lot of people don't trust God with their future. They think He will tell them to do something they won't want to do. Well, be assured, though the Lord may give you an assignment you never thought of before, it will still line up with the desires He already placed in your heart.

Since I love to teach, I never considered being a writer. Now, I get to teach the book I wrote to people everywhere! God fulfilled the desire of my heart. He will give you something to line up with your desires too!

Very quickly, there is one last vital point I need to share with you to help you recognize the revelation of your Expected End. Do you remember, in the beginning of this chapter, we talked about recognizing God's voice? I told you that, if you didn't act on your revelation, you would feel as though you were perishing. Well, the opposite is also true. When you take action on the thoughts God is sending you, you will experience a **supernatural** joy! Let me explain.

Again, look at the parable of the talents, but this time look at the response the master gave to the two servants who promptly acted on their assignments.

*"His master replied, 'Well done, good and faithful servant! **Come and share in your master's happiness!'"**

Because of their obedience to pursue their assignments, the two servants were invited to come and share in their *"master's happiness!"* What does this mean? The master's happiness is different from ordinary happiness. It is the joy God gets when His children finally take action on what He created them to be! Their Expected End! Because it is called the **master's** happiness, it also means it is supernatural! When you are obedient to act on your assignment you get to *"come and share"* in it!

Supernatural joy is your indicator you've taken possession of your Expected End! I remember when the Lord instructed me to form a corporate prayer team in my prison. The team's job, He said, would be to follow Jeremiah's instruction to pray for our place of exile. When the Lord first told me this, I naturally assumed He wanted me to lead the group, but, instead, He instructed me to put a woman named Remi in charge.

Although Remi had already served nine years in prison, she still had no clue as to her future God assignment. One thing for sure was that she possessed a huge anointing for prayer. The Lord revealed to me that He wanted Remi placed in her royal position in the group because she needed to be there in order to receive the revelation of her Expected End.

So, quickly the team gathered, setting Remi as its leader. Immediately, God began to make powerful things happen in those meetings. Even more exciting though was what happened to Remi herself. Just a few weeks after the group started, I saw her out on the yard. I will never forget what she said as we talked about the project. Literally bursting at the seams, she cried out, **"Oh the joy, Sister Kate, the joy!"**

At that moment, I knew Remi was experiencing God's supernatural joy because she had finally taken possession of what would become her Expected End!

When I obeyed God by starting to write this book, I was immediately filled with a joy I never felt before! When you experience the *"master's happiness"* for the first time, you will know it because it will be unlike anything you ever experienced! When you get it, you will know you heard from God correctly and have taken possession of your Expected End!

In Jeremiah's letter to the captives, God promises to send, **toward you,** the revelation of your assignment. *"For I know the thoughts I think toward you... to give you an Expected End."*

Make sure you are in the right position to receive your revelation, and then trust God to keep His promise to give it to you. Once your revelation comes, act on it. Don't stop your pursuit until you accomplish what God is directing you to do. I guarantee that if you do these things, you will experience life in more abundance than you could ever dream!

Lesson Seventeen

1. One of the explanations why people miss the revelation of their Expected End is contained in this verse. *"And who knows but that you have come to royal **position** for such a time as this?"* What does this verse mean in connection to receiving the revelation of your Expected End? Are you currently involved in the fellowship?

2. *"For if you **remain silent** at this time... **you will perish...**"* (Esther 4:14). According to this verse, if God is speaking to you but you take no action on what He is moving you to do, it will feel as though you are literally_____. (Fill in the blank.) Have you been feeling this way lately? What recurring thoughts or ideas have you been ignoring that could possibly be from God?

3. According to this verse what was Esther's first reaction to the revelation of her assignment? *"...any man or woman who approaches the king in the inner court without being summoned the king has but one law: that he be put to death... thirty days have passed since I was called to go to the king"* (Esther 4:11).

4. When God reveals your assignment, will you be ready to "die" to your own desires and lay everything aside to pursue it?

5. In the parable of the talents, the Bible says the master gave his servants talents, *"each according to his ability."* Do you believe God will give you no more than you can handle? Do you believe He will supernaturally enable you to complete the job He assigns you?

6. According to these verses, what happens when you do not act on the revelation of your Expected End? *"...Do not think that because you are in the king's house you alone of all the Jews will escape. **For if you remain silent at this time, relief and deliverance for the Jews will arise from another place,** but you and your father's family will perish"* (Esther 4:13-14). *"...'You wicked, lazy servant! ...**Take the talent from him and give it to the one who has the ten talents"*** (Matthew 25:26, 28).

7. Laziness is one of the main reasons why people miss out on their Expected End. Write out the following verses in the space below. *'You wicked, **lazy** servant! ...Take the talent from him and give it to the one who has the ten talents"* (Matthew 25:26, 28). In what areas of your life are you showing signs of laziness? Are you willing to lose your future over it?

8. Write out Proverbs 3:5-6 and explain what it means concerning the revelation of your Expected End?

9. If you fail to take action on the thoughts God sends you concerning your Expected End, you will feel as though you are literally perishing in a dry and desert land. Well, the opposite is also true. When you take action on the thoughts God is sending, you will experience a **supernatural joy!** In the parable of the talents, look at the response the master gave to the two servants who **promptly** acted on their assignments. *"His master replied, 'Well done, good and faithful servant! ...Come and share in your master's happiness!'"* (Matthew 25:21).

Supernatural joy is your indicator that you have taken possession of your Expected End! When you have been obedient to act on your assignment you will be blessed to, *"come and share in your _____!"* (Fill in the blank.)

CHAPTER EIGHTEEN

A Prophecy against Babylon

"...Elam, attack! Media, lay siege! ...Babylon has fallen, has fallen!"
Isaiah 21:2, 9

I laid in my cell late one September night meditating on the Lord. It had been my nightly ritual for years. That night, I had a question for Him and was waiting in expectation for His answer.

A year earlier, I was given a 13-year sentence after two years of fighting in the federal courts. The night of my sentencing, I called my Mom and Dad to give them the bad news. That's when we discussed the possibility of appealing my case.

"Only God knows if we would win or lose," I said to them. "So I want to hear from Him before we do anything." They both agreed with me, and then we made a pact to go before the Lord individually to seek His will concerning the appeal.

"I want to do whatever God tells us to do," were my parting words, "even if it means doing all my time." Even though this comment may have made me sound like Miss Super Christian, deep inside I was really hoping I wouldn't have to go through with it. I didn't want to stay behind bars for 13 years. I was praying God would agree with me. Fortunately, I didn't need to wait long for His answer because that night He spoke to me in a dream.

As I slept, I saw a black screen in my mind with the word ELAM printed across it in big white letters. When I awoke, the vision was so clear it was as if a picture imprinted on my memory.

Immediately, I called my parents to question them about Elam. When my Mom told me Elam was Persia, the light bulb went on. I knew from my studies of the Old Testament captivities that Persia, under the leadership of King Cyrus, freed the Israelites from imprisonment in Babylon. This realization sent a jolt through my body! I knew right then God was about to tell me something wonderful!

Armed with the Scripture references on Elam, I returned to my cell, and then began searching the Bible for God's directions. When I reached Isaiah 21, I knew He answered my question about the appeal.

The first thing I saw was the heading of the chapter as it literally leaped out at me. *"A Prophecy against Babylon"*, it declared. Because I knew Babylon represented the judicial system, the words that followed looked 10 feet tall and bulletproof. The Scripture said,

*"...Elam, **attack! Media, lay siege!** ...Babylon has fallen, has fallen!"*

God's answer to my question was clear. If we filed an appeal, Babylon would fall and we would win. Waves of relief and excitement flowed through me as I ran to call my folks with the news. A few days later, they too received their confirmations, at which point my mother, who now sounded very confident, said,

"We believe so much that what the Lord said will come to pass, we are going to put our money where our mouth is!" Then, backing up her statement, my folks used the funds they received from the sale of their property to hire an appeal lawyer.

Now, it was a year later. I believed I was going home, but when? I felt like something was going to happen in November, which was right around the corner. So, late that September night as I lay in my bunk, I silently conversed with the Father about my release.

"Lord, you know from the day I walked into this prison I stepped out in faith to tell everyone about Elam and how you are going to allow me to go home."

As I ended this thought, I briefly paused to contemplate how I would pop my question. "I feel like something is going to happen in November." I continued, and then paused again before hesitantly asking, "Am I right? Boy, I sure hope so."

Feeling cocky, I had been shooting off my mouth, telling everybody I would be home in time to eat Thanksgiving dinner, which was on November 22nd. As I stopped my dialog with the Lord for a minute, my mind drifted away to picture myself arriving triumphantly, home in time to cook turkey for Mom and Dad. Since federal bureau policy stated no one got released on holidays or weekends, I would be let out on the day before Thanksgiving - November 21st.

"Okay, Lord." I thought as I turned my attention back to Him. "If I will be home in time for Thanksgiving dinner, tell me how many days are there from now until November 21st?"

I immediately stopped and got quiet. In the stillness of my mind, I heard, "57." At first I thought, "That was just me," but then I decided to check. I sat up in my bunk and began to count off the days on my calendar. When I reached 57, I landed on November 21st and my heart jumped!

"Maybe I made a mistake," I thought. So, taking a very deep breath, I slowly recounted again to make sure. Again, I landed on November 21st.

"It can't be!" Now my breath was coming quicker, but I still forced myself to count very slowly as I tried a third time. When I came up to the 21st again, I thought, "There is no way I could have calculated this number so quickly on my own. It has to be the Holy Spirit." As the realization started to sink in, I freaked! I was going home!!

The next day, I ran out to tell everybody in the facility what the Lord said, but only a small handful believed. The rest looked at me with amusement. By the end of the day, the news spread like wildfire until the majority of the inmates were laughing at me. I pretended not to care; but deep inside I did, so that evening I went to the Lord again.

"Father, they think I'm nuts but I can't stop telling everyone what You're doing." At this, I opened up my Bible. It fell on Jeremiah 20. As I read though the chapter, lo and behold, there was Jeremiah going through exactly what I was.

"...I am ridiculed all day long; everyone mocks me... the word of the Lord has brought me insult and reproach... But if I say, 'I will not mention Him or speak any more in His name,' His word is in my heart like a fire, a fire shut up in my bones. I am weary of holding it in; indeed, I cannot" (Jeremiah 20:7-9).

Just like Jeremiah, the word God spoke was bringing me ridicule. Nevertheless, it felt like a fire in my bones that I could not contain.

"I don't care what they say Lord," I thought, as I straightened my shoulders in resolve. "I believe You and I am going to continue to tell everyone what You said." As I read through the rest of Jeremiah's complaint, I felt I was in good company.

The next 57 days were very interesting to say the least. I totally crawled out on a limb by keeping up the testimony no matter what was said about me. God, in turn, encouraged me on by giving me dozens of confirmations that indeed He was going to fulfill His word.

As the day approached, you could literally see people holding their breath. Even the unbelievers were anxious. It was as if they wanted it to happen so they would have a reason to believe. Then the staff got wind of it and one of the counselors in my housing unit called me into her office.

"So, I heard you think you're leaving on November 21st," she inquired. I don't think it. I know it.", I replied.

"How's that, when you have a 13-year sentence?" she retorted.

So, I began to tell her what God said. Her response was to immediately call for two officers to escort me to the facility's psychiatrist.

"So you're hearing voices?" the psychiatrist began, her eyes narrowing as she looked at me skeptically.

"Not exactly," I replied. "I hear God giving me direction."

"So you think you're hearing God's voice, huh?" Her tone confirming that she now believed I was stone-cold crazy.

"Well, I don't hear some big booming voice saying 'Katie, this is God!'" I said, imitating a deep rumbling tone. "I hear the direction of the Holy Spirit talking to me in my mind. I understand the voice of God directing me through Scripture."

"Oh, really?" Her voice trailed off. Right then, I could see disbelief written all over her face. "Do you think you need to be put in suicide watch?" she prodded.

"Absolutely not!" I said firmly. "You don't believe what I'm saying because you just don't believe. It's a God-thing, you know!"

She continued to grill me for another half an hour before finally scheduling me for an appointment on November 21st. "When it doesn't happen," she said, explaining why she set the 21st as my appointment date, "you will need to come in and see me."

As I walked away from her office, my last thought was "Whatever!"

November 21st finally did arrive. My roommate Angie and I were ending a 3-day fast. It was past noon and I was in the middle of a prayer meeting when suddenly one of the sisters came running in to tell me that the Records office just paged me!

"This is it!" I screamed and jumped up to run out of the Chapel with another sister at my side. Weeping, we made our way down to Records. As we rounded the corner, I practically burst though their door! "You paged me!?!" I said, out of breath.

The woman there looked up from the desk and shook her head. "No, it must have been a mistake." she said rather casually. Oh, and what a cruel mistake it was. The rest of the day passed and nothing happened – nothing! I was devastated. All kinds of emotions and questions raced through me. What went wrong? I was so sure I had heard from the Lord. In fact, the more I thought about it, the more I realized I wasn't even upset about not going home. My main concern was being able to get an accurate Word from God. Without this, I knew everything else would be lost.

Then there was the ministry. Would my error hurt other peoples' faith? How could I continue to lead the women after this? I began to question whether or not I was even qualified. Did I dare go on teaching, instructing and guiding the flock?

Immediately, the enemy took advantage of what was happening. He swooped in and tried to set up a stronghold in my mind, whispering that everything I ever heard from the Lord, every prophetic word, the direction for the ministry and even the word about my appeal was wrong. Did this mean my parents spent tens of thousands of dollars based on a lie?

The mind onslaught continued. I felt angry with God. Why didn't He warn me? Why didn't He protect me from the enemy's deception? Now I was suspicious of the voice inside of me that I'd come to cherish and depend on. Confused and overwhelmed,

I began to reject any guidance He was giving me. After all, where was it really coming from? I began to falter.

"My God, where can I go?" I was broken. The rug was pulled out from underneath me, but it was too late. I was hooked: Hooked on God. Even though I was in total despair, I knew I had no choice but to press on. So, I made a stand. I continued to go to prayer and church even though I didn't feel like it. I even went back to teaching Bible studies, pushing aside the shame.

Six months went by. The ministry was really showing fruit. I was teaching *The Captivity Series* and the Lord began to instruct me to write down the Series. But, fear and doubt, aided by the memory of my recent catastrophe, were working against me. However, though I steadfastly tried to ignore what God was now telling me to do, I soon realized I would be completely miserable until I obeyed. So finally, I gave in to the revelation of what would become my Expected End and that's when it happened.

I called my Mom and Dad one night and they told me we won our appeal. I was going back to court for re-sentencing! When I heard it, I was so stunned I asked them to repeat it back to me three times. After I hung up the phone, the Lord informed me He just brought the word about Elam to pass, which meant I heard and understood Him correctly. I gained confidence.

Three months later, I was flown to court for re-sentencing via the infamous Con-Air. When I arrived, my attorney told me the Prosecutor was going to try to give us even more time, but again the Lord spoke. *"All who rage against you will be as nothing,"* He said and, as always, He was exactly right! When it was all done, I came out of court with seven years removed from my sentence! God said Babylon would fall and indeed it did. I was going home!

As I was flying back to my facility to complete the remainder of my time, I couldn't help but wonder what was up with the number 57 and the November 21st date. Exactly what would my new outdate be after they recalculated my sentence? As I sat there, shackled to my seat, watching the billowing clouds outside my window, I felt an excitement rise up in my spirit. Could it be I heard from Him correctly but had the wrong interpretation? Either way, I would soon find out.

Two agonizing months went by before my papers were completed. Finally, the day arrived when my case manager called me in to give me my new date. As she handed me the paper, I grasped a hold of it, paused and then looked down. When I saw the words "Projected Release Date, **November...**" I drew in a sharp breath,

"Could it be?" I thought, as a scream started to rise up in my throat, but when I saw the date that followed, my scream was cut short.

"November 23rd!?!" I said out loud in dismay. "I can't believe it." I shook my head and looked at the paper again to make sure. Indeed, there was the number 23 staring up at me mockingly. My new counselor, unaware of what was going on, looked confused. Not feeling in the least like I wanted to explain it to her, I spun around and shuffled away mumbling,

"Why, Lord, why?"

As I entered my cell, I threw the paper down in disgust. "November 23rd." I said to my roommate Angie as I climbed up onto her bunk to look at her calendar. "I was off by two days, Ang."

"November 23rd? What's up with that?" She asked bewildered.

"The 23rd lands on a Saturday." I continued, after I found the page where November was located, "This means they will release me on Friday the 22nd."

Frustrated, I let out a sharp exhale. "Only one day off!" I huffed. "One day off," Angie repeated back, sounding equally baffled.

I sat there stunned for a while, staring blankly at the calendar with a thousand questions running through my mind. Then suddenly the realization hit me. I was looking at 2002, the wrong year!! Quickly, I turned to the back of the calendar in search of the following year but it wasn't there.

"Ang!" I snapped, "where is 2003 on this thing!"

"It doesn't have one." she replied with a questioning look.

Taking no time to explain, I leapt off the top bunk, scooped up my release paper and tore down the hallway to a friend's cell. When I burst through their door, everyone inside jumped.

"Do you have a 2003 calendar?" I screamed frantically.

"What's going on?" She said hesitantly, as she took down the calendar from her board to hand it to me.

"I got my new outdate!" I said breathlessly, fingers riffling through the pages.

Instantly, the room got quiet because they all knew what was going on. Shaking, I finally reached the month of November, and then slid my pointer finger quickly across the glossy page to the 23rd.

"Well?" Somebody finally asked.

"Oh thank You, Jesus!!" I whispered, barely breathing.

"November 23rd falls on a Sunday," I announced to everyone, "which means..." I paused again feeling almost oxygen-deprived. "They will have to release me on Friday, the **21st of November!!**"

When I spoke the last sentence, my volume reached a crescendo, and then the room exploded as I screamed out the date. Instantly, everybody leapt up to clasp hold of each other in a big group hug. Then, everyone started jumping and swaying, non-stop until we all came tumbling out the door.

As I broke free from the circle to run back to tell Angie, everyone followed. On the way there, we created such a stir people started coming out of their rooms to see what was causing the ruckus. Within minutes, the news spread again like wildfire, but this time to the Glory of God! It was only later after things calmed down a bit that I realized November 21, 2003, would be my **57th** month in captivity. God makes NO mistakes!!

Lesson Eighteen

1. Has God given you a promise? Is so, write the details in the space below. Include the Scriptures He spoke to you concerning that promise.

2. Does it sometimes seem that your promise is never going to come to pass? Why?

3. What things are making you doubt?

4. Whom are you going to believe? Your doubts, or the Word of God, and the promises He has spoken to you?

5. Ask God right now to affirm His promises to you. Pray and then get quiet. Let the Lord speak a Scripture into your mind to confirm what He said will come to pass. If you get a Scripture that totally speaks to you, write it down, memorize it and pray it often. However, if you get a Scripture that doesn't exist or make sense, you are only hearing your own thoughts, not God's.

CHAPTER NINETEEN

BABYLON HAS FALLEN

<u>From Jeremiah's Letter to the Exiles</u>

"'You will seek me and find me when you seek me with all your heart. I will be found by you,' declares the LORD, 'and will bring you back from captivity. I will gather you from all the nations and places where I have banished you,' declares the Lord, 'and will bring you back to the place from which I have carried you into exile.'"
Jeremiah 29:13-14

"The LORD will carry out his purpose, his decree against the people of Babylon. You who live by many waters and are rich in treasures, your end has come, the time for you to be cut off."
Jeremiah 51:12-13

In 539 B.C., the city of Babylon, which was situated on the Euphrates River, fell to King Cyrus of Persia and his armies. The Greek historian Herodotus tells us that Cyrus, seeing the impossibility of breaking through the massive walls of Babylon, decided to go under them instead. First, he positioned some of his forces at the place where the river went under the city's walls. Then, he took the rest of his army upstream where they dug a canal in order to reroute the flow of the Euphrates into a nearby marsh. When the river level lowered enough, it allowed Cyrus's men to march right in under the walls to take Babylon by surprise.

Chapter 5 of the book of Daniel tells us what was simultaneously taking place inside the city that night. The Babylonians, very confident their massive fortress was in no danger, were engaged in a festival of drinking and dancing when the sneak attack occurred. King Belshazzar was throwing a banquet for a thousand of his lords. During the festivities, he brought out the gold and silver vessels taken from the temple in Jerusalem so his guests could drink from them. As the partygoers toasted their pagan gods with the sacred vessels, a hand appeared from the supernatural realm to write a message on the wall. The message said God had numbered the days of Belshazzar's reign and brought it to an end. His kingdom was to be divided between the Medes and the Persians. That very night Cyrus marched in, Belshazzar was slain, and then Darius the Mede took over as king. The mighty Babylon fell in one night. The people of Israel were then released from their captivity.

Centuries earlier, the prophet Isaiah foretold of this fateful night with frightening accuracy:

"The mournful, inspired prediction (a burden to be lifted up) concerning the Desert of the Sea [which was Babylon after great dams were raised to control the waters of the

Euphrates River]... As whirlwinds in the South (the Negeb) sweep through, so it [the judgment of God by hostile armies] comes from the desert, from a terrible land... Go up, O Elam! Besiege, O Media! All the sighing [caused by Babylon's ruthless oppressions] I will cause to cease [says the Lord]... My mind reels and wanders, horror terrifies me. [In my mind's eye I am at the feast of Belshazzar. I see the defilement of the golden vessels taken from God's temple, I watch the handwriting appear on the wall -- I know that Babylon's great king is to be slain.]... They prepare the table, they spread the rugs, [and having] set the watchers [the revelers take no other precaution], they eat, they drink. Arise, you princes, and oil your shields [for your deadly foe is at your gates]! ...And he [the watchman] tells [what it foretells]: Babylon has fallen, has fallen..." (Isaiah 21:1-2, 4-5, 9 AMP).

This prophecy from Isaiah, spoken hundreds of years before the fall of Babylon, proves the release of the Israelite captives didn't happen by chance, but rather by the hand of God through the vehicle of a king. Who was this king?

Cyrus the Great (580-529 B.C.) founded Persia by uniting two Iranian tribes, the Medes and the Persians. During his lifetime, Cyrus conquered many nations, including Babylon in October of 539 B.C. However, Cyrus was more than just a great king and conqueror. The Bible says he was God's chosen instrument to deliver the Israelites from captivity. Two hundred years before Cyrus was ever born, the prophet Isaiah called him by name and foretold of the mission God planned for his life.

"This is what the LORD says to his anointed, to Cyrus, whose right hand I take hold of to subdue nations before him and to strip kings of their armor, to open doors before him so that gates will not be shut: I will go before you and will level the mountains; I will break down gates of bronze and cut through bars of iron... He will rebuild my city and set my exiles free..." (Isaiah 45:1-2, 13).

Breaking down gates of bronze and cutting through bars of iron! Cyrus was called to pull off a literal jailbreak and then help the Israelites rebuild Jerusalem. In fact, after Cyrus defeated Babylon then freed the captives, he issued this landmine proclamation concerning Israel's return home.

*"In the first year of Cyrus king of Persia, **in order to fulfill the word of the LORD spoken by Jeremiah, the LORD moved the heart of Cyrus** king of Persia to make a proclamation throughout his realm and put it in writing: This is what Cyrus king of Persia says: 'The Lord, the God of heaven, has given me all the kingdoms of the earth and he has appointed me to build a temple for him at Jerusalem in Judah. **Anyone of his people among you - may his God be with him, and let him go up to Jerusalem in Judah and build the temple of the LORD...'"** (Ezra 1:1-3).

After Babylon's defeat, Cyrus helped the captives to reclaim their home. In 537 B.C., at the king's command, 40,000 Jews left Babylon loaded down with goods and precious things to be used in rebuilding Jerusalem. The Scripture above says God moved the heart of Cyrus so the promise in Jeremiah's letter could be fulfilled.

"'...when you seek me with all your heart. I will be found by you,' declares the Lord, 'and will bring you back from captivity... and will bring you back to the place from which I have carried you into exile'" (Jeremiah 29:13-14).

God kept His promise to bring the Israelites home by raising up a deliverer to set them free! Many of you are ready to go home. You've fulfilled God's purposes for your time so you believe He is going to uphold your cause to get you out! Well, let me tell you the secret to securing your freedom: Listen to God and follow His directions!

I first learned about King Cyrus through a personal word the Lord gave me about my case. After I lost my trial, my parents and I began to look for a new lawyer. Though we had a few choices to pick from, the Lord kept leading us in the direction of a man named Billy Blackburn.

"He is Cyrus." The Lord told me.

"What do you mean, Lord?" I asked. At which point the Father led me to these Scriptures about Cyrus.

"...The LORD's chosen ally will carry out his purpose against Babylon; his arm will be against the Babylonians. I, even I, have spoken; yes, I have called him. I will bring him, and he will succeed in his mission" (Isaiah 48:14-15).

After I read this verse, I knew the Lord was saying Billy was my Cyrus. He was the man God chose to redeem me from my captivity.

Let me tell you the reason why I won my case. My family and I let God direct the whole process! We filed an appeal because God told us to file. We hired the lawyer God told us to hire. We listened to the Lord, obeyed His instructions and were victorious!

God has a detailed plan concerning your release. Look at Cyrus. The Lord gave him a specific plan on how to defeat Babylon: Go under the walls instead of trying to go through them! Because Cyrus followed this plan, he didn't lose a single man that night. Babylon totally surrendered to Him without a fight! This is how easy things are when God is in it!

God's plans always work. Doesn't this make you wonder why so few people ever consult Him concerning their release? I've known countless prisoners who wasted their time and money on inadequate lawyers and worthless motions. I've seen people get their hopes up just to be totally disappointed because they believed the latest rumors on the yard about some "miracle" law being passed. Why, I've even known inmates who fell for a scheme that they could buy their way out of prison! How heartbreaking, especially when, all the while, God's plan could have easily procured their freedom.

You must consult God for His battle strategy. Look again at the Scripture about Cyrus succeeding in his mission against the Babylonians. Then look closely at the verse that follows.

"...The LORD's chosen ally will carry out His purpose against Babylon; his arm will be against the Babylonians. I, even I, have spoken; yes, I have called him. I will bring him, and he will succeed in his mission... **'I am the LORD your God, who teaches you what is best for you, who directs you in the way you should go. If only you had paid attention to my commands, your peace would have been like a river...'"** (Isaiah 48:14-15, 17-18).

Only the Lord can direct you as to which way to go concerning your release. If you listen to Him, you will experience victory! However, if you listen to yourself or do what the world tells you to do, you will fail.

You must learn to seek the Lord to listen for His direction. As you sit before Him in prayer and during your study of the Scriptures, He will give you detailed instructions on what course you are to follow. Don't worry that you won't be able to understand the revelation because the Holy Spirit and your knowledge of Israel's captivity will help you. Believe me, it isn't as difficult as you think. Take my case, for example. When I asked if I should appeal my sentence, God gave me the following Scripture:

"Elam, attack! Media, lay siege! ...Babylon has fallen, has fallen!"

What would this mean to you now that you know Israel's history? Probably the same thing it meant to me. Attack in the Appeals Court and win! God wants you to understand the revelation. If you didn't, it wouldn't help you!

If you've already filed motions or taken some kind of action without seeking God first, don't despair. You can still ask for God's help. Then, once you receive His battle strategy, follow it through, even if it goes against the world's advice. Remember that God's path, not man's, will lead you to victory. You must let the Lord pick the weapons of your redemption. If you simply trust and obey Him, He will raise up a Cyrus for you, as He did for Israel. Then, He will fulfill His wonderful plans for your life.

Lesson Nineteen

1. Jeremiah 29:13-14 says, *"You will seek me and find me when you seek me with all your heart. I will be found by you,' declares the Lord, 'and will bring you back from captivity. I will gather you from all the nations and places where I have banished you,' declares the Lord, 'and will bring you back to the place from which I have carried you into exile.'"* When you seek God with all your heart by building a relationship with Him and becoming what He created you to be, the Scripture above says that He will, *"bring you back from* _____ *"* (Fill in the blank.)

2. How much time were you given on your sentence? Are you fighting your case? Do you need the time of God's favor?

3. King Cyrus overthrew Babylon in one night, freed the Israelite captives and helped them rebuild Jerusalem. Isaiah 48 tells us Cyrus, *"...the LORD'S chosen ally will carry out His purpose against Babylon; his arm will be against the Babylonians. I, even I, have spoken; yes, I have called him. I will bring him, and he will succeed in his mission."* Why do you think Cyrus succeeded in His mission?

4. Isaiah 48:17-18 says, *"...I am the LORD your God, who teaches you what is best for you, who directs you in the way you should go. If only you had paid attention to my commands, your peace would have been like a river..."* According to Scripture, where should you seek guidance concerning your case? God or man?

5. Have you been pursuing options for your case without consulting the Lord? Why?

6. Are you in need of God's favor concerning your sentence? Begin spending quiet time with the Father. Pray, read the Scriptures, and listen for Him to speak to you through His Word. God will give you a detailed plan to follow. Trust Him and do as He, not man, instructs, and you will experience victory!

CHAPTER TWENTY

THE PERFECT MATCH

"When the Lord brought back the captives [who returned] to Zion, we were like those who dream [it seemed so unreal]. Then were our mouths filled with laughter, and our tongues with singing. Then they said among the nations, The Lord has done great things for them. The Lord has done great things for us! We are glad!"
Psalm 126:1-3 AMP

Almost five years passed since I was first arrested. Even though I was supposed to be in prison for seven more, I was out! I had just completed six months in a halfway house and was now sitting in the office staring at the calendar board hanging on the wall. My name and the word "RELEASE" were written in the block marked "November 21, 2003!" My miracle date was coming to pass! After signing the papers, I stepped out the door. The sun never seemed so bright, especially in comparison to a few months earlier.

When I first arrived at the halfway house, I quickly realized being there was much harder than being in the joint. So much so, there were days I wished I were back inside! Prison had been a mountaintop experience for me as far as God was concerned, but, obviously, things on the outside were different. Now, it felt like I'd been thrown off the mountain and kicked to the curb. My spiritual life was in some kind of a nightmarish holding pattern as my once daily discipline of study was flushed, then replaced by the hustle and bustle of reality. All this caused me to flounder like a fish out of water on a hot day, slapping against the pavement and gasping for breath.

As far as the book was concerned, I hadn't scratched out a single word since I got out. I could feel the tension in my spirit because of it. Soon, I caught myself breaking the rules, and then getting write-ups at the halfway house. It seemed the farther I got from God and my purpose, the more those kinds of infractions happened.

It wasn't hard to see if I continued on the path I was on, I would eventually get into real trouble. Feeling desperate, I decided to make a comeback. However, in the free world, there wasn't time for anything but survival, not to mention study and prayer. By the way things were going though; I knew if I didn't start putting God first, everything else in my life would slowly fall apart.

So, I began by taking my Bible on the bus so I could use the time to read. I also carried around my dad's out-of-date cassette player so I could listen to praise tapes. I even decided I would pray while doing any kind of activity, like walking or showering.

Surprisingly, as I followed through with those little efforts, I began to feel a real difference. Finally, I even got to the point where I was ready to work on the book. When I did, I could feel the fire start to rage inside of me again!

Soon the power of my Expected End began to manifest in my life. I felt no temptation to return to drugs or my old lifestyle! I was filled with an excitement and joy beyond explanation! Everywhere I went, I received favor and God began to move for me in surprising ways. Three warrants popped up, threatening to send me back to prison, but they were totally dismissed! A fine I had paid to the court was returned to me! I got a job singing and selling music in a karaoke store. Then I was given some money, which, along with my savings, I used to buy a new car. Plus, during this time, I just "happened" to bump into people who were in prison ministry. My life was going so well it seemed like I was charmed!

Through it all though, God made it obvious that the amazing amount of "luck" I was experiencing was directly connected to Him and my assignment. The more I put my mission first, the more He made sure I was taken care of in a big way. In fact, the stuff happening to me was so amazing it felt like I was in Vegas and I was on a roll! Then **he** showed up.

A few months before my release, I was placed on home confinement. I was living with my parents while still attending treatment classes at the halfway house. Robert Souza was in one of my classes. At first, I didn't really notice him until, one day, in response to a question; he espoused a very biblically accurate answer. "Huh, a theologian," I thought disdainfully. Nevertheless, I felt a connection with him, as he was obviously the only other Christian in the group.

Weeks later, when I arrived late for class, I discovered the only seat left was the one next to Robert. As we began the day's assignment, I let my eyes drift over to see how he was doing. I found he had answered every question from a biblical standpoint. Admiring his desire to make God the center of his life, I reached over and wrote a big "A plus" at the top of his paper.

When class was over, I got up to hurry out the door, only to have him quickly catch up to me.

"I would like to discuss the biblical text with you sometime," he said, as we reached the curb.

"Sure," I responded, without thinking. "I'll give you my number." As soon as I said it, however, I wanted to take it back.

Robert, though, looked more than pleased. "Ok, I'll give you mine too!" he said happily, grinning from ear to ear.

Seeing his response, I forced myself to smile back. "Let me go to my car and get a pen," I said, straining to cover the tone of regret now in my voice. Then, I turned away from him quickly so he wouldn't see me lose it as I ran across the street.

"What have you done?" I mumbled to myself as I dug through the car's console. Though he seemed like a nice guy, he wasn't my type. Plus, I definitely didn't have time for a relationship. When I returned with the pen to exchange numbers, all I could think was, "Please Lord, don't have him call."

Unfortunately, he did. The very next morning, Robert left a very short, but polite, message on my service. "Now what are you going to do?" I thought, scolding myself. "You can't be rude and just ignore him."

Thinking it over, I decided I would call and pray he wouldn't answer so I could just leave a message. Thus, when I dialed, then his service picked up, I let out a loud, "Praise God!" Then, at the beep, I told him I was sorry I missed his call. I also told him I wouldn't be available to talk for the rest of the day. Then, in closing, I said,

"But, it was nice to hear from you anyway; goodbye!" After I hung up, I thought to myself, "Good job, maybe this will dissuade him."

But, no such luck. He called the very next day and I mistakenly answered my phone without first looking to see who it was. "Good morning. This is Robert," he said, voice thick with a Massachusetts accent. "How are you?"

I replied, "Fine, thank you," while kicking myself.

We chatted for a few minutes, then he told me he would call later, which he did and I answered, but only out of pure guilt. This time though, as we talked, something happened. Robert's conversation began to irresistibly draw me as it was about my favorite subject – God. As I listened to Robert, it became very apparent he was deeply studied in the Word. The more he talked, the more I marveled at his knowledge; but I also couldn't help but feel he was looking for much more than biblical conversation.

"Thank God we are not allowed to be around each other," I thought with relief. Because of our status as ex-felons, we were not to have contact outside our classes. To do so would get us violated, then sent back to prison. This, I realized, was my saving grace, as it would prevent my new friend from becoming any more than this. Unfortunately, I was soon to learn that nothing would deter Robert Souza from his chosen course.

A few days later, while I was at work, he called as usual and said with a giggle, "Good morning, Mrs. Souza!"

"Excuse me!" I replied in astonishment.

To which he promptly responded, "Well, the Lord told me you are my wife."

At this announcement, my defenses immediately went up. "I don't think so." I said sarcastically; but then, realizing my harshness, tried to explain, "I'm not planning on getting married because I have lots of things to do."

"Like what?" he asked in an inquisitive, but demanding, tone.

I suddenly felt cornered. How do you tell someone they don't fit into the big picture of your life? Not wanting to injure him, I tried a broader statement. "Well, I'm on a mission from God." I replied.

"And what exactly does that mean?" he inquired further.

So, I gave in. I began to tell him about the book. I didn't mention it before because I figured he wouldn't get it. In fact, most people didn't. Whenever I tried to explain what I was doing, no one seemed to understand; but in order to be polite, they would always respond with some obligatory comment like, "Well isn't that wonderful" or "Good for you."

Now, somehow feeling like I owed it to Robert, I tried to explain it as best I could and he tried to understand as best he could. However, he didn't quite get it, which is what I expected. I didn't anticipate what he did next though.

A few hours later, Robert walked into my work, set a backpack on the counter; then, to avoid further rule infractions of our probation, he turned around and walked out. From the parking lot, he called me from his cell phone to explain.

"I brought you my Bible, a concordance and some study materials to help you write your book!"

"How sweet!" I told him, and truly meant it. At the same time, however, I couldn't help but think how I didn't need his Bible and concordance since I owned dozens of my own. This, of course, I kept to myself and just continued to thank him for his wonderful gesture. After I hung up, I thought that, since I wasn't going to use any of his materials, I would just hold on to them until I saw him again, if ever.

Work was dead that day with not a soul coming into the karaoke store. As the hours crept by, the Lord began to bug me to look at Robert's Bible. At first, I resisted, and then finally gave in out of sheer boredom. Grabbing his backpack, I set it up on the counter, and looked inside.

The Bible was leather bound and in immaculate condition for its age. When I took it out to leaf through the pages, I was stunned. They were filled with handwritten symbols indicating different topics. In the margins were tiny handwritten notes, so perfectly printed it looked as though a miniature typewriter did them. Robert served 17 years, nine of it in intense study of the Scriptures. I was now reading through the product of all those years.

As I continued to look through his Bible, I unexpectedly began to weep. As the tears started flowing down my face, I glanced at the opened page to see what the text was, then my eyes landed on a verse that hit me like a stone,

"...It is not good that man should be alone" (Genesis 2:18 NKJV).

"Oh, my!" I said aloud, a little concerned; then looked down again to further investigate. Unfortunately, what I saw only made it worse.

"...He brought her to the man" (Genesis 2:22 NKJV).

"Whoa! Definitely not funny, Lord," I said, looking up toward heaven while pointing at the offending Scripture.

At this, I closed Robert's Bible, mopped the remaining saltwater off my face with a tissue from my pocket, and then paused to assess what just happened. Since I didn't believe in coincidence, it didn't look too good for me; but, maybe this time, it was just that – coincidence.

"Well, there is only one way to find out." I thought, as I boldly opened up his Bible again. However, when I looked down, I realized my situation had gotten worse.

"...let her be the woman whom the Lord has appointed for my master's son" (Genesis 24:44 NKJV).

The sight of this sobering declaration sent shock waves running through me! Was it God's plan to give me to Robert? If so, in my opinion, there was only one-way to deal with this plan. Ignore it and ignore him!

However, Robert wouldn't go away. Since we couldn't be around each other and I was still living at home, he decided he would spend time with my parents whenever I was at work. So, night after night, while I was at the store, he wooed them with his charm and homemade spaghetti.

"He is not playing fair!" I declared to my mom; but my father was not in agreement, especially after he consumed bowl after bowl of the delicious bribe.

Then one night, Bobby called me and began to push the marriage thing again.

Fed up, I said rather callously, "Listen, the Lord hasn't told me you are my husband. So, until He does, you just need to drop it!"

The silence on the other end of the line indicated I went too far. The conversation was over. When I hung up, I felt as though I literally stabbed Bobby in the heart. The next morning though, he called, seemingly unaffected, with an announcement.

"The Lord said He is going to tell you that I am your husband."

"Ha!" I snorted. "Is that right?"

"Yes," he replied, quite sure of himself. "And He is going to do it 'soon, and very soon'!"

"Well, we'll see about that," I countered in a sarcastic tone. Conversation over, I hung up feeling very sure I would be hearing no such thing, neither sooner nor later.

About a week after his call, I was up all night with my mom. She suffered with intense pain for over 20 years, but this night was particularly bad. When she finally did get to sleep, I too was exhausted, but only got a few hours of rest before I woke up again. After looking at the clock, then seeing it was still early, I decided to go back to bed for a short nap.

When I drifted off to sleep, I got a vision. In my mind, I could see myself writing a note to Bobby on top of a cocoa brown suede tie. The note said, "I have a message in my heart for you." As I watched the pen writing out the message over and over, I suddenly snapped into consciousness. I woke myself up from saying the words out loud in my sleep.

"What was that, Lord?" I inquired. Then I laid back down to mull it over until I fell asleep again.

A couple of hours later, I arose and decided to run on the treadmill. I was using the time to pray and talk with the Lord. When I was in a full run, praying against my mom's illness, the Lord interrupted me, then replayed in my mind the vision I'd seen earlier. As I again watched my hand write out the words, "I have a message in my heart for you," I silently asked the Lord what those words meant.

"OK, Father," I began, "what was the mess..."; but, before I could even think the word "message" all the way out, He interrupted by answering rather loudly with, "I DO!"

His words hit me like a freight train. Groaning and saying out loud, "No, no, no, Lord!" I staggered, grasped hold of the handrail, then, put my feet on the outer edge of the treadmill, leaving the belt whining at high speeds beneath me.

"No, this can't be!" I protested again; but the Lord's words were still echoing in my head loud and clear, "I DO, I DO, I DO."

Gritting my teeth, I pressed down with extra force on the treadmill's stop button to emphasize my frustration. The machine then ground down to a halt, leaving me huffing, puffing and standing there stunned, with salty sweat dripping off my face.

I didn't even know Robert, and he didn't know me. So, how could he possibly fit into my life with all my plans for the book and the ministry? The Lord had to be wrong this time. So, feeling defiant, I planted my hands on my hips and, looking up to heaven, said,

"You are really going to have to prove this one for me to believe it."

Fortunately, a lightning bolt didn't strike me down, but instead I instantly felt wave after wave of the Holy Spirit run through me. I was now hot and sweaty, but with major goose bumps from head to toe. God was going to show me all right, and in a big way.

Though at first I didn't tell Bobby what happened, he acted like he knew. He became a man possessed, insisting we ask probation for permission to be married. It didn't matter to him that what he was requesting was forbidden. An unseen force, the Holy Spirit, was guiding him to do what I knew now was God's perfect will.

From this point on, God put it into high gear to bring His Word to pass. After a very brief scuffle with probation, they miraculously gave in. In April of 2004, only four months after my release and six months after Bobby's, we were married. Then, just six months later, we were supernaturally enabled to buy our first home. I can remember feeling totally amazed by God the day we moved in. Though our new house was filled with every kind of provision, the only thing in it we paid for was a TV!

After that, only a few more months went by before God instructed my husband to start his own business. The Lord promised Bobby He would prosper the company so that I could be freed up to pursue my assignment. Now, Bobby and I were partners in getting the mission completed! Immediately, my husband's company took off, generating three times more income than we had previously! I then quit my full-time job, finished the book and birthed "Expected End Ministries."

Everything happened so quickly it left people wondering how two ex-cons could be doing so well. Of course, I knew the answer; God was in it. His perfect plan was being worked out through us. Bobby and I were now sharing love and chasing after the mission together. The Lord was blessing us with a life more abundant than we could ever imagine!

As I sat back to look at what God was doing, I realized how grateful I was that I listened to Him and not myself. I may not have known Robert Souza, but God did. He knew we would become the perfect match for each other in love and for our Kingdom purpose. Later on in a conversation with my mom and dad, it was brought up that, when they got married, my dad wore a cocoa brown suede coat, a perfect match to Bobby's tie.

Lesson Twenty

1. Write down plans the Lord has put in your heart. Describe any details or insights you've received concerning those plans.

2. What things do you think will be difficult for you once you get out? Why?

3. Write down what you think you can do to overcome those difficulties.

CHAPTER TWENTY-ONE

"Thus says Cyrus king of Persia...Whoever is among you of all His people, may his God be with him, and let him go up to Jerusalem in Judah and rebuild the house of the Lord... Then rose up the heads of the fathers' houses of Judah and Benjamin, and the priests and Levites, with all those whose spirits God had stirred up, to go up to rebuild the house of the Lord in Jerusalem... The whole congregation numbered 42,360."
Ezra 1: 2, 3, 5; 2:64 AMP

In 538 B.C., King Cyrus made his historical proclamation for the Israelite captives to go home. The Bible says, in response to the king's edict, God stirred up the spirit of over 42,000 people to want to return to Jerusalem to rebuild the house of the Lord. Led by Zerubbabel, heir to the throne of David, and Jeshua, the high priest, the first wave of exiles prepared to go home to pursue their mission. To assist them, the Israelites who remained in Babylon donated gold, livestock and gifts to the project. Plus, King Cyrus gave back the sacred vessels stolen from the original temple. When the exiles walked out of Babylon, they possessed everything they needed to begin their assignment!

In the next few chapters, we are going to follow the stories of each of the three groups of returning exiles. As we study the trials and triumphs the ancient prisoners faced upon their release, you are going to discover many valuable truths to help you to make it on the outside and enable you to successfully take possession of your Expected End!

First Things First

There were three very important practices the first group of returnees instituted after their release from prison. First, Israel began the practice of tithing as soon as they arrived in Jerusalem. Second, the people gathered for fellowship after they got settled into their towns. Then, third, the exiles reinstituted the daily sacrifices according to what was written in Scripture. These three practices significantly contributed to Israel's success when they got out. Therefore, they are also vital to your success once you are in the free world.

Now, let's examine them one by one. The very first thing the exiles did when they walked into Jerusalem was to give a **tithe.** The Scripture says, *"When they arrived at the house of the LORD in Jerusalem, some of the heads of the families gave freewill offerings toward the rebuilding of the house of God on its site. According to their ability they gave to the treasury for this work 61,000 drachmas of gold, 5,000 minas of silver and*

100 priestly garments. The priests, the Levites... settled in their own towns ...and the rest of the Israelites settled in their towns" (Ezra 2:68-70).

Immediately upon their entry into Jerusalem, the exiles tithed. In fact, even though the people just walked 900 miles from Babylon, they still went out of their way to tithe before they even unpacked and settled into their towns! This particular act of giving was of such great significance it was even recorded a second time in chapter 7 of the book of Nehemiah!

Why did the exiles make tithing their first priority upon arriving home? The Israelites understood the vast importance of tithing. They knew it was God's way to test their faith and obedience. It was also the vehicle God used to bring increase to His people. Israel was in the free world now, and were about to face many challenges. In order to make it, they needed to rely totally on God. This is why they gave their tithe as soon as they walked in the gate. They wanted to show the Lord through their obedience, that they trusted Him to provide for all their needs.

Most of you were probably very irresponsible with your money when you were on the outside. Well, once you get released again, money is going to play a major part in your life. In order for you to make it in the free world, you are going to need to trust God and learn how to handle your money His way.

You see, God, not your employer, will be the true source of your income once you get out. This is fortunate because most regular jobs don't pay well. You see, God is able to provide you with much more than just your hourly wage. He can cause you to receive gifts and unexpected funds. He can enable you to buy a new home or start a new business. The Lord can even give you an idea for an invention. God owns the wealth of the world, so as long as you are being obedient to handle your finances His way, He will bless and increase you. He will even give you creative ways to generate income. So, what is God's way of handling finances?

God's priority for your money is to use it to build His Kingdom. The returned exiles knew this. Just look at where they tithed their money.

*"When they arrived at the house of the LORD in Jerusalem, some of the heads of the families gave freewill offerings **toward the rebuilding of the house of God on its site.**"*

Israel understood God's priority for their money was His Kingdom. This is why they put their money into rebuilding the temple. The Lord wants you to get involved in building His Kingdom also. One way to do this is by faithfully giving to your church and other Christian programs. When you choose to make God's priorities first in your finances, He, in turn, will bless and increase you. One of the reasons my husband and I are given more than we could ask for is because we continue to financially partner with the Father to build His Kingdom on earth.

Now, exactly how much of your money does the Lord want you to give? Well, in the Old Testament, the word tithe means 10%. Tithing a tenth of your income is a good yardstick to measure your giving by. However, there will be times when the Lord will also ask you to give above your ordinary gift. In fact, every time He made a major financial move for my husband and me, He always asked us to give an **extra** gift over our regular amount.

The first time it happened was just weeks before we got married. I remember my husband-to-be almost fainted when the Lord told me to give away 30% of my total paychecks for three months. At that time, we needed every dime, so, of course, we thought we couldn't afford it. However, when I finally chose to be obedient to write out the check, I received a surprise check in the mail for the same amount later that day! That year, this one special tithe brought us more blessings than I can count! In fact, I would need to write another chapter just to be able to list all the incredible things God did for us through it.

The next time the Lord asked us to give an extra tithe was the same morning He told my husband to start his new business. This time, the Lord instructed us to give $40 a month for a year to a Christian Television Network. Because we were obedient the business immediately took off! We became more financially secure then we had ever been. Then I was able to quit my full-time job to pursue my mission!

Tithing is vital to your personal relationship with God and to your financial security. It is also an intricate aspect of your Expected End. **God will always connect your giving to your** assignment - like when He instructed us to give the $40 dollars. You see, God uses the tithe to test you to see if you will give when He tells you, where He tells you and the amount He tells you. The Lord requires this kind of obedience because money will always be involved in completing your Expected End. Whether you need ten dollars to print some flyers or ten thousand to print a book, it takes money to spread the gospel and, sometimes, lots of it. God will supply for all the needs of your mission, but only if you learn to be a good steward over His money! Remember, the Bible says he who is faithful over a few things will be put in charge of many. (Matthew 25:21)

Tithing is a powerful biblical principle. Because it really works, you will face a lot of tests when it is time for you to tithe. Will you give God the whole 10% and on a consistent basis? Will you obey Him when He instructs you to give a special gift? Will you give the amount He asks for or will you just give what you think you can afford? Will you trust Him and not be afraid to give even when you think you don't have it? There will be times when it looks like you can't afford to tithe, but, in reality, you can't afford not to!

Also, don't worry about not having anything to give when you first get out. Look at the amount the exiles tithed when they first returned home. Scripture says, *"According to their ability they gave to the treasury for this work."* Israel gave according to what they were able to give! So when you get out, if you have a buck in your pocket and you tithe ten cents, God is going to honor it! In fact, you will be shocked at what God does with your one dime!

Okay, now let's go back to the story of the returned exiles to look at the second practice they instituted after arriving home in Jerusalem. The Scripture says, *"When the seventh month came and the Israelites were settled in the towns, the people gathered together as one man to Jerusalem"* (Ezra 3:1 AMP).

After Israel settled in, they came together for fellowship. It is important to note that, although the exiles were spread apart in their own towns, they didn't stay isolated from each other. Instead, they chose to go **out of their way** to gather for spiritual, physical and moral support.

When you get out, you need to do the same. Once you return home and get settled, you need to go out of your way to find a church; then you must faithfully attend it. Why is this so important?

Well, fellowship offers many things. The first is the Word of God. The Word contains power to correct you when you are in sin. It also enables you to overcome temptation. In the free world, you will face many trials; so it will be absolutely necessary for you to be exposed to sound biblical teaching on a regular basis. This teaching is what will keep you grounded and on the right path.

The fellowship is also intended to be your support system. The church is made up of people who are anointed to give biblical guidance, which will enable you to navigate through your daily trials. When godly people surround you, you will be less likely to backslide or suffer a collision with sin. Think about it. It is hard to continue sinning when believers are surrounding you! I knew an ex-con who did a lot of time during which he developed a deep relationship with God. Nevertheless, when he got out, he went right back to his old habits. In fact, for years, he struggled in vain against his drug addictions. Well, one of the reasons why he never totally overcame them was because he refused to seek the help of the church. Whenever he fell, because he was embarrassed or just being rebellious, he would rely on his own strength to overcome his addiction instead of seeking help from other Christians. Unfortunately, because his strength was never enough, he failed repeatedly. He kept the church elders out of his struggle so his sin remained hidden, enabling him to continue backsliding for years. This is one of the reasons why you must surround yourself with believers. They will keep you accountable.

The fellowship is also the place where you will walk out your Expected End! You see, God gives you an idea and expects you to develop it; however, your **mission can only be fully executed within a body of believers.** Let me show you proof from the Scriptures. First, look at this example from the first wave of returned exiles.

*"In the second month of the second year after their arrival at the house of God in Jerusalem, Zerubbabel son of Shealtiel, Jeshua son of Jozadak **and the rest of the brothers (the priests and the Levites and all who had returned from the captivity to Jerusalem) began the work..."** (Ezra 3:8).*

Zerubbabel and Jeshua were in charge of rebuilding the temple, but they didn't attempt to execute the project on their own, they got help. The Scripture says *"the rest of the brothers"* joined in with them to complete the work.

In the second wave of returnees, we see the same principle. Ezra, the scribe, was on a mission to go to Jerusalem to restore temple worship and teach the returned exiles the Word of God. Well, right when he was getting ready to leave Babylon, he noticed there was no one in his group sanctified to carry out the temple service. At this discovery, Ezra realized his mission could go no further. He knew, before he could leave Babylon, he needed to find qualified men to come with him. The Scripture says,

*"Because the gracious hand of our God was on us, they brought us Sherebiah, a capable man, from the descendants of Mahli son of Levi... Sherebiah's sons and brothers... Hashabiah, together with Jeshaiah... and his brothers and nephews... They also brought 220 of the temple servants - **a body that David and the officials had established to assist the Levites..."** (Ezra 8:18-20).*

Like the above Scripture says, the body was established by God to assist in carrying out the assignment. Ezra realized and understood that, if he attempted to go any further without the body, his mission would fail!

You will need the help of the fellowship to complete your assignment. Look at another example from the third wave of returned exiles. Nehemiah came from Babylon on a mission to repair Jerusalem's broken down wall. Right after he arrived home, the Bible says he called all of the exiles together to begin building. The following Scriptures show how the people combined their efforts to complete the project.

*"Then Eliashib the high priest rose up with his brethren the priests and built the Sheep Gate... and **next to** him...the men of Jericho built. **Next to** [them] Zaccur son of Imri built... **After him** the Levites... **After him** the priests..."* (Nehemiah 3:1-2, 17, 22 AMP).

In chapter 3 of Nehemiah, the phrases *"next to"* and *"after him"* are used over two dozen times to describe how each group worked on a section of the wall *"next to"* their brothers who were working on another section. That "chain" linked the exiles together as one body. Because they combined their efforts, the wall was completed in only 52 days!

During the first three years of my assignment, I was pretty much on my own because I was writing the book. As I got closer to publishing and actually carrying out the mission, God began to bring people *"next to"* me to help. One by one, those whom God appointed joined in to assist in completing the assignment. Since each person possessed talents I didn't, we were a thoroughly equipped body, able to tackle every situation! I couldn't have completed my mission if it weren't for the help of those believers!

Your survival, your spiritual health and the fulfillment of your Expected End are within the fellowship. You must get into a church once you get out of prison. However, though you may be planning on attending church after your release, you will find when the rubber meets the road, it's not as easy as it sounds.

After we got out, my husband and I struggled on many occasions to keep up our church attendance. Whether we were busy, tired, or just being flaky, there were moments when we would stray. Each time we did, though, we suffered not only spiritually, but also in our daily lives along with our marriage relationship.

When you get out, your life will be busy and stressful. In the free world, you will have hundreds of responsibilities to take care of. Your house will always need to be cleaned. The kids will always need to be taken care of. Some emergency will always seem to arise. Life in general will provide dozens of excuses for you to miss fellowship.

However, when your church attendance declines, so will your spiritual life. The more you skip fellowship, the more you will be open to temptation. Eventually, you will even find yourself getting into bad situations, then violating and going back to prison! The fellowship is there to guide you through your messes and, more importantly, to help you avoid them! It is also the place where you will fulfill your Expected End! So, when you get out, make church a regular part of your life, no matter what your schedule.

So, after Israel tithed, then gathered together as one man in Jerusalem to fellowship, what did they do next? The Bible says they built an altar to the Lord, making offerings on it according to what was written in Scripture.

*"...and they built the altar of the God of Israel to offer burnt offerings upon it, as it is written in the instructions of Moses the man of God... and they offered burnt offerings on it to the Lord **morning and evening**. They kept also the Feast of Tabernacles, as it was written, and offered the **daily** burnt offering... And after that, the **continual** burnt offering... From the first day of the seventh month they began to offer burnt offerings to the Lord, but the foundation of the temple was not yet laid"* (Ezra 3:2-6 AMP).

Not long after the exiles returned to Jerusalem, they began the practice of offering sacrifices to God according to the instructions contained in Scripture. The Bible says the people made these offerings, *"morning and evening," "daily"* and on a *"continual"* basis. In other words, these sacrifices were given regularly. Why is this so important?

In Chapter Eleven of this study, we talked about the vital necessity of developing a Christ-centered lifestyle. This is the practice of spending daily time with God, praying and studying the Scriptures. Although you, hopefully, began this practice while you were on the inside, you will have to work to reestablish it as a part of your routine after you are released.

Your personal relationship with the Father must be your first priority over everything else. Your whole life changes when you get out, but your daily habit of spending time with God needs to remain the same. Unfortunately, you will find, like I did, that this is most difficult to do. The world's demands can be so overwhelming; you will think you have no time to spend with God. However, if you do not regularly offer up this sacrifice, you will slowly decay in your spiritual walk until you fall into a deadly trap.

Your future success on the outside will depend on you living Christ-centered. Every day in the real world, you will need to make dozens of choices. Only through regular study and prayer will you be able to successfully navigate through those decisions.

When my husband and I got out, there were many times when we lapsed in our daily reading. When this happened, though, we would force ourselves to make adjustments in our lifestyle in order to get back on track. Unfortunately, a lot of other ex-cons we knew were not doing the same. They weren't staying committed to their daily study time, and, as a result, were being violated, and sent back to prison!

It has always amazed me how reading a few chapters in your Bible can have such a powerful influence on your life! After you are released, you must do as the returned exiles did; follow after the Word *"morning and evening, daily* and *continually."* Do not let yourself think you have no time to study, because your survival will depend on it! **You must choose to make time!** If you have to wake up earlier or go to bed later, do it. If you need to, listen to the Bible on CD in your car or take your Bible with you on the bus. Heaven forbid you might even have to drop a half-hour of your TV time to get your reading in!

Even the pursuit of your Expected End must take second place to your daily time with the Father. After my release, there were a few months when I convinced myself that, because I was writing the book, I didn't need to get in my personal time with God. Well, I was wrong and even my writing started to suffer because of it.

Your Expected End cannot substitute for your prayer and study time. The ancient Israelites knew it. Look again at the Scripture in Ezra, *"From the first day of the seventh month they began to offer burnt offerings to the Lord, **but the foundation of the temple was not yet laid."*** Rebuilding the temple was Israel's Expected End, but they understood their daily sacrifices to God were more important! This is why they reinstituted them before they laid the temple foundation! Once you get out, you need to reestablish your daily time with God. Make it your first priority over everything else, including your mission.

Because the returned exiles started their new lives by tithing, fellowshipping and making daily sacrifices, they got off on the right foot. Unfortunately, they soon ran into some serious problems. In the next chapter, we are going to see what Israel did wrong and how you can avoid doing the same.

Lesson Twenty-One

1. According to Scripture, what is one of the first things the Israelites did upon their arrival home? *"When they arrived at the house of the LORD in Jerusalem, some of the heads of the families gave freewill offerings toward the rebuilding of the house of God on its site. According to their ability they gave to the treasury..."* (Ezra 2:68-69).

2. Why is tithing important? How much should you tithe on a personal level? In what ways is tithing connected to your Expected End?

3. According to Scripture, what else did the Israelites do when they returned home? *"When the seventh month came and the Israelites were in the towns, the people gathered together as one man to Jerusalem"* (Ezra 3:1 AMP).

4. Why is attending church and fellowship so important? What does fellowship have to do with your Expected End?

5. According to Scripture, what is the third thing the Israelites did upon their return home? *"...and they built the altar of the God of Israel to offer burnt offerings upon it, as it is written in the instructions of Moses the man of God ...and they offered burnt offerings on it to the Lord **morning and evening.** They kept also the Feast of Tabernacles, as it was written, and offered the **daily** burnt offerings... And after that, the **continual** burnt offering..."* (Ezra 3:2-6 AMP).

6. Why is it so important to continue your habit of living a Christ-centered life once you get out? In pursuing your Expected End, do you see why it is so vital not to neglect your personal time with the Lord each day? Name two practices that are essential in living Christ-centered.

CHAPTER TWENTY-TWO

THE FIRST PROBLEMS

"In the second month of the second year after their arrival at the house of God in Jerusalem, Zerubbabel son of Shealtiel, Jeshua son of Jozadak and the rest of their brothers (the priest and the Levites and all who had returned from captivity to Jerusalem) began the work, appointing Levites twenty years of age and older to supervise the building of the house of the Lord."
Ezra 3:8

The returned exiles started off in the free world the right way, by tithing, fellowshipping and making daily sacrifices to God. Once they established those practices, they began working on their assignment to rebuild the temple. However, when the enemies of the Jews heard about the building project, they came with evil motives in their hearts and offered to help the exiles build.

Wisely, Israel refused their offer; but then the Bible says that the enemies of Israel, *"...set out to discourage the people of Judah and to make them afraid to go on building. They hired counselors to work against them and frustrate their plans during the entire reign of Cyrus king of Persia and down to the reign of Darius king of Persia"* (Ezra 4:4-5).

Israel's enemies wasted no time in launching a full assault against the exiles. Counselors were hired to intimidate the returnees and frustrate their plans. Attempts were made to discourage the temple builders and put fear in them. What was the purpose of these attacks against the Israelites? The Scripture above tells us, **"to make them afraid to go on building."** Each assault was an attempt to get the exiles to **stop working on their Expected End!**

Fortunately, the Israelites didn't stop, or at least not right away. The attacks continued for years, wearing the exiles down, but not causing them to totally quit. However, when the enemies of the Jews wrote a letter to Artaxerxes, the king of Persia, filled with accusations against Israel, the work on the temple was completely halted. Let's look at what was said about the exiles in this letter to the king:

"...we are sending this message to inform the king, so that a search may be made in the archives of your predecessors. In these records you will find that this city is a rebellious city, troublesome to kings and provinces, a place of rebellion from ancient times. That is why this city was destroyed. We inform the king that if this city is built and its walls are restored, you will be left with nothing in Trans-Euphrates" (Ezra 4:14-16).

The letter stated Israel had a bad record and a history of rebellion, which was why they were sent into captivity. The letter even went on to insinuate that, if the exiles were allowed to rebuild Jerusalem, they would rebel again! These statements were obviously an attempt to use Israel's "ex-felon" status against them. Unfortunately, the attempt was successful. After reading the accusations, King Artaxerxes sent back this reply:

"Now issue an order to these men to stop work, so that this city will not be rebuilt until I so order. Be careful not to neglect this matter. Why let this threat grow, to the detriment of the royal interests?" (Ezra 4:21-22).

The ploy on the part of Israel's enemies worked. The king ordered the exiles to stop building. The Scripture confirms, *"Thus the work on the house of God in Jerusalem came to a standstill..."* (Ezra 4:24).

The attacks achieved the purpose for which they were sent: to stop the exiles from completing their mission! Why was the enemy so driven to do this? **Because the most powerful weapon against the kingdom of darkness is the person who is pursuing their Expected End!**

This is why satan does not want you to complete your assignment. He knows, if you do, it will critically damage his kingdom. In order to get you to quit, he will use every avenue available to wear you out, make you afraid and discourage you. The devil will work through people to frustrate your plans. He will turn ordinary circumstances against you. He will even use your past record to attack your credibility, just like the enemies of ancient Israel did in their letter to the king. Because you are pursuing your mission, **you will be attacked!** The question is, "How will you handle it?"

What did Israel do? They held out for a while, but then finally buckled. Because of Artaxerxes' reply, the Bible says, *"...the work on the house of God in Jerusalem came to a standstill..."*

The Israelites allowed the attacks to bring their mission to a halt. In fact, the work on the temple stopped for over 18 years! During this time, the exiles retreated to their own homes to focus on rebuilding them instead. Though the people probably justified quitting because they were ordered by the king to do so, nowhere in Scripture does it say **God** told them to quit. Unfortunately, they did anyway, and for 18 long years!

From this point on, the exiles' lives took a turn for the worse. Their harvests stopped coming in. Their wages disappeared, and prosperity totally ceased. The years of abundance were gone. Drought and famine took their place. By the time 18 years passed, the returnees were desperately struggling to make it. What happened? God sent the prophet Haggai to the people with this powerful answer:

"In the second year of Darius king [of Persia], in the sixth month... the word of the Lord came by means of Haggai the prophet [in Jerusalem after the Babylonian captivity] to Zerubbabel son of Shealtiel, governor of Judah, and to Joshua son of Jehozadak, the high priest, saying, thus says the Lord of hosts: These people say, The time is not yet come that

the Lord's house should be rebuilt [although Cyrus had ordered it done eighteen years before].

"Then came the word of the Lord by Haggai the prophet, saying, Is it time for you yourselves to dwell in your paneled houses while this house [of the Lord] lies in ruins? Now therefore thus says the Lord of hosts: Consider your ways and set your mind on what has come to you.

"You have sown much, but you have reaped little; you eat, but you do not have enough; you drink, but you do not have your fill; you clothe yourselves, but no one is warm; and he who earns wages has earned them to put them in a bag with holes in it.

"Thus says the Lord of hosts: **Consider your ways (your previous and present conduct) and how you have fared.** Go up to the hill country and bring lumber and rebuild [My] house, and I will take pleasure in it and I will be glorified, says the Lord [by accepting it as done for My glory and by displaying My glory in it].

"You looked for much [harvest], and behold, it came to little; and even when you brought that home, I blew it away. Why? says the Lord of hosts. **Because of My house, which lies waste while you yourselves run each man to his own house [eager to build and adorn it].**

"Therefore the heavens above you [for your sake] withhold the dew, and the earth withholds its produce. And I have called for a drought upon the land and the hill country, upon the grain, the fresh wine, the oil, upon what the ground brings forth, upon men and cattle, and upon all the [wearisome] toil of [men's] hands" (Haggai 1:1-11 AMP).

In this message, the Lord told the exiles to *"consider your ways (your previous and present conduct) and how you have fared."* Previously, Israel was doing very well. When they first got out of prison, they faithfully pursued their assignment and were very prosperous. However, later they weren't faring well at all. In fact, they were experiencing total famine. Why? The Scripture explains, *"because of My house, which lies waste..."*

God called for a drought on the Israelites because **they ceased working on their Expected End.** This is one of the major reasons why people go back to prison. They stop pursuing their God-given purpose, so they fail. Do you remember this verse from Chapter Sixteen?

"The LORD foils the plans of the nations; He thwarts the purposes of the peoples. But the plans of the LORD stand firm forever, the purposes of His heart through all generations" (Psalm 33:10-11).

The Bible makes it clear. Only God's plans for your life will succeed. So, if you exchange His purposes for your own, you will fail no matter what you try to do. In fact, God Himself will cause you to fail, just like He did to the ancient exiles. This is why you must continue to pursue your assignment after you get out! If you stop working on it, you will fail. Then you will eventually go back to what you did before your arrest. When this happens, you will either go back to prison or end up living a miserable, half-full existence.

Unfortunately, faithfully pursuing your assignment when you get out will be very difficult. Just like the ancient exiles, you will face many assaults from the enemy, whose goal is to stop you from completing your mission. You will be attacked mentally, physically, emotionally and spiritually. Your credibility and your record will be questioned. You will even have to fight against yourself because you will be tempted to focus on your own needs instead of the needs of your Expected End.

Let me give you an example. When my husband and I first bought our house, we needed to be very careful we didn't do as the ancient exiles did, *"...run each man to his own house [eager to build and adorn it]."* It was so tempting to spend all our money and time fixing up our new home. Unfortunately, there were moments when our focus turned away from our Expected End, but, thank God, we realized that, to continue would mean our doom!

We all have the tendency to do as Haggai said, *"dwell in your paneled houses while this house [of the Lord] lies in ruins. "* This is what the ancient exiles did. They stopped working on the temple, and focused on rebuilding their homes. They exchanged God's purpose for their own priorities, so God caused them to fail. Anyone can fall into this trap! When you get out, you must remember to avoid it at all costs.

Don't get me wrong; God doesn't want you to neglect your own personal needs, but He does require that you faithfully see to the needs of your mission. This is why you must learn to make sufficient time for both your assignment and your household. Just remember that, if you put God first, He, in turn, will give you everything else you need!

What happened when the Lord, through the prophet Haggai, commanded the people to return to their work on the temple?

*"NOW THE prophets, Haggai and Zechariah son [grandson] of Iddo, prophesied to the Jews in Judah and Jerusalem in the name of the God of Israel, Whose [Spirit] was upon them. Then rose up Zerubbabel son of Shealtiel [heir to the throne of Judah] and Jeshua son of Jozadak and began to build the house of God in Jerusalem ...And the elders of the Jews **built and prospered** through the prophesying of Haggai the prophet and Zechariah son of Iddo. **They finished their building as commanded by the God of Israel**..."* (Ezra 5:1-2; 6:14 AMP).

When the exiles heard Haggai's message, they rose up to complete their assignment! Notice the Scripture says Israel *"built and prospered."* When it comes to your Expected End, these two things go hand-in-hand. As long as you continue to faithfully work on your mission, God will make sure you prosper.

The Recurring Problem

What other problems did Israel face when they arrived home? The second major issue they dealt with was the repeat of the sin that caused them to go into captivity in the first place. It was the problem of intermingling with the people of foreign nations.

In 458 B.C., the second wave of captives returned to Jerusalem. This group was led by the scribe, Ezra, whose mission it was to restore temple service and teach the returned exiles the Word of God. Unfortunately, upon his arrival home, Ezra encountered a problem. The exiles were intermingling with the people of the other nations around them. The Bible says,

"...The Israelites and the priests and Levites have not separated themselves from the peoples of the lands, but have committed the abominations of the Canaanites..." (Ezra 9:1 AMP).

The returnees had married foreign women and were following after their idolatrous practices! This was a very dangerous situation for the exiles to be in. Do you remember why? In Chapter Four, we discussed the two sins that led Israel into exile, which were:

"...They worshiped other gods and followed the practices of the other nations the LORD had driven out before them..." (2 Kings 17:7-8). When the Israelites first crossed over into Canaan to conquer it, the Lord commanded them to destroy all the land's inhabitants. Unfortunately, the Israelites didn't fully obey. They eventually intermingled with the people who were left alive. Those survivors led the Jews into committing idolatry, which, according to the Bible, is why God sent His people into captivity in the first place. Now, here were the returned exiles repeating this same sin again! When Ezra found out, he was appalled. Going to God in prayer, he said,

"Since the days of our fathers we have been exceedingly guilty; ...and ...have been delivered into ...captivity ...and after all that has come upon us for our evil deeds ...shall we break Your commandments again and intermarry with the peoples who practice these abominations?" (Ezra 9:7, 13-14 AMP).

Ezra knew the ramifications of what Israel was involved in. The people were setting themselves up to go back into captivity again!

As I mentioned before, the recidivism rate for ex-cons is 70%. That means seven out of 10 people released from prison will return. I'll bet if you talk to someone who violated, they will tell you that one of the reasons why they were sent back was because they started hanging out with the wrong people **again.** That is why God does not want you to intermingle with the people of the world.

Intermingling is a behavior ex-cons throughout history have repeated over and over. You don't believe me? Twenty-five years after the first incident during Ezra's time, a second situation arose when Nehemiah returned home to Jerusalem. Nehemiah says, *"In those days also I saw Jews who had married wives from Ashdod, Ammon, and Moab. And their children spoke half in the speech of Ashdod, and could not speak the Hebrew, but in the language of each people"* (Nehemiah 13:23-24 AMP).

Again, the returned exiles were marrying people who practiced idolatry! Repeatedly, the Jews put their freedom and futures in jeopardy by intermingling with the people of other nations. This was a reoccurring problem that continually plagued the Israelites. How did Ezra and Nehemiah handle this problem? The same way you should. **Severely!** Let's look at their examples.

When Ezra found out about the relationships the exiles became involved in, he called for them to assemble in Jerusalem within three days time. He even said that whoever didn't show up, would have all their land and possessions taken away from them. So, by the third day, all of Israel was assembled; and then Ezra stood up saying,

*"...You have been unfaithful; you have married foreign women, adding to Israel's guilt. Now make confession to the LORD, the God of your fathers, and do His will. **Separate yourselves from the peoples around you and from your foreign wives"*** (Ezra 10:10-11).

Ezra commanded the men to sever their relationships with the people of the world. This meant sending away the wives and children they loved! Now, this was a severe course of action to take. However, Ezra knew it was the only possible solution.

Nehemiah responded to the problem of intermingling with equal, if not more, severity than Ezra. The Bible tells us what he did to the Israelites who formed the wrong associations.

"I rebuked them and called curses down on them. I beat some of the men and pulled out their hair. I made them take an oath in God's name and said: 'You are not to give your daughters in marriage to their sons, nor are you to take their daughters in marriage for your sons or for yourselves'" (Nehemiah 13:25).

Nehemiah responded to the problem of intermingling by beating up the men who were involved! He even pulled out their hair, and called down curses on them! (I'll bet one of those curses was the curse of captivity!) Plus, Nehemiah made them swear to God that they wouldn't allow their children to commit the same trespass. Though Nehemiah's response was intense, once again it was the only way to handle the situation!

Sometimes it takes drastic measures to end sin. If you let yourself get involved with the people of the world, you will eventually need to cut them off or else end up back in prison. Do yourself a favor; don't even allow those kinds of associations to get started! If you do, it will be hard for you to separate from them later on. Think about how those men felt when Ezra commanded them to send away their wives and children! What a horrible thing to have to do. It was absolutely necessary, however, or Israel would go back into captivity again!

How did the exiles respond when Ezra told them they needed to separate themselves from their families? The Bible records them as saying, *"You are right! We must do as you say"* (Ezra 10:12).

Israel responded with immediate obedience, therefore the fierce anger of the Lord was turned away from them. If you get entangled with the people of the world again, you will need to handle the situation like the ancient exiles did. If you don't, you will lose your freedom and destroy your life.

In this chapter, we looked at the many challenges the first and second wave of exiles faced upon their release. Because they mishandled a lot of their situations, it took them nearly 40 years to complete their work on the temple! In the next chapter, we are going to look at Nehemiah to see how he handled the challenges of his Expected End and why it only took him 52 days to complete it.

1. Once the first wave of returned exiles began rebuilding the temple, their enemies *"set out to discourage the people of Judah and to make them afraid to go on building. They hired counselors to work against them and frustrate their plans during the entire reign of Cyrus king of Persia and down to the reign of Darius king of Persia"* (Ezra 4:4-5). According to these Scriptures, what was the enemy's goal?

2. How did Israel eventually respond to these attacks? Write out Ezra 4:24 in the space below.

3. When the returned exiles stopped pursuing God's plan for their life in order to pursue their own wants and desires, God called for a drought on all the work of their hands. What does Psalm 33:10-11 signify in connection with this situation?

4. According to this next Scripture, what is the second thing the Israelites did wrong when they returned home *"...the Israelites and the priests and Levites have not separated themselves from the peoples of the lands, but have committed the abominations of the Canaanites"* (Ezra 9:1 AMP).

5. The sin of intermingling is one of the reasons why Israel was taken into captivity. When you go home, you must keep yourself separate from people who could wrongly influence you. If you don't, you could end up in _____ again! (Fill in the blank.)

CHAPTER TWENTY-THREE

"...Then I prayed to the God of heaven, and I answered the king, 'If it pleases the king and if your servant has found favor in his sight, let him send me to the city in Judah where my fathers are buried so I can rebuild it.'"
Nehemiah 2:4-5

In 445 B.C., Nehemiah set out from Jerusalem armed with a mission. While still in the land of captivity, he received word Jerusalem's walls were broken down, leaving the city unprotected. Devastated, he received royal sanctioning from the king of Persia to go and repair them. After Nehemiah arrived in Jerusalem, he secretly rode around its perimeter to inspect the damaged wall, and then rallied the exiles together to begin the work of rebuilding.

However, when Sanballat the Horonite, Tobiah the Ammonite official, and Geshem the Arab heard Jerusalem's defensive wall was being built, they launched multiple attacks against Nehemiah and the exiles. At first, the conflicts were just verbal ones, but soon they escalated to where the very lives of the exiles were threatened! Thankfully, even though the conditions were severe, the people still finished the wall in an amazingly short time! In fact, the whole project took only 52 days, which, compared to the 40 years it took to finish the temple, was nothing short of miraculous!

What did Nehemiah and his group do differently than the first wave of exiles that enabled them to complete their assignment in such a short span of time? In this chapter, we will explore Nehemiah's technique and look at the way he handled problem circumstances while pursuing his Expected End.

Nehemiah's Reliance on God through Prayer

First and foremost, Nehemiah was a great man of prayer. He possessed a deep understanding that prayer **really** works. From the very beginning of his mission, Nehemiah relied on prayer to get his goal accomplished. In fact, as early as verse 4 in Chapter 1 of the book of Nehemiah, we see he is already praying for his assignment. At this time, Nehemiah was still in the land of captivity, acting as King Artaxerxes's cupbearer. When he heard Jerusalem's walls and gates were broken down, he immediately went before the Lord in prayer to seek His help.

"When I heard these things, I sat down and wept. For some days I mourned and fasted and prayed before the God of heaven. Then I said: 'Oh LORD, God of heaven, the great and awesome God, Who keeps His covenant of love with those who love Him and obey His commands, let Your ear be attentive and Your eyes open to hear the prayer Your servant

*is praying before You day and night for Your servants, the people of Israel.... They are Your servants and Your people, whom You redeemed by Your great strength and Your mighty hand. O Lord, let Your ear be attentive to the prayer of this servant and to the prayer of Your servants who delight in revering Your name. **Give Your servant success today by granting him favor in the presence of this man'"** (Nehemiah 1:4-6, 10-11).*

This man Nehemiah was referring to was King Artaxerxes. In order for Nehemiah to be able to go home to rebuild Jerusalem's wall, he needed favor from the king. Fortunately, Nehemiah knew prayer could get him this favor. In fact, Nehemiah relied so much on the power of prayer to get the favor he needed, the Bible even records him as silently praying to God **right in the middle** of making his request to the king.

*"The king said to me, 'What is it you want?' **Then I prayed to the God of heaven, and I answered the king..."** (Nehemiah 2:4-5).*

What was the result of Nehemiah's prayer? He received the favor he was asking for. The Bible says Artaxerxes not only gave him permission to go to Jerusalem, but also provided him with a letter of safe conduct home and a cavalry to escort him there! Artaxerxes even gave Nehemiah permission to take from the king's forest any timber and beams he would need to set up the gates of Jerusalem. (Nehemiah 2:6-9)

Right from the start, Nehemiah incorporated prayer into **every** aspect of his Expected End. The Scripture above proves this. When Nehemiah shot a silent prayer to God right in the middle of his conversation with the king, it showed Nehemiah's total dependence on prayer to get his mission done! In fact, you will see Nehemiah, throughout this chapter, consistently *"pray without ceasing"* (1 Thessalonians 5:17 NKJV). That means to pray everywhere you go, at all times, even right in the middle of your conversations!

Prayer was a habit for Nehemiah. So much so, **he automatically responded to every situation with prayer,** like in his conversation with Artaxerxes. Obviously, Nehemiah's prayer technique worked because he obtained everything he needed to go on his mission!

Fortunately, by the time I began my assignment, I already started to develop the habit of praying without ceasing. Since then, I've realized how much this habit was responsible for my success. I've always prayed for every aspect of my mission and I've never lacked anything I've needed to complete it! When I needed favor, I prayed and God opened doors of opportunity! When I was attacked, I prayed for supernatural help and got it. When I needed provisions, I prayed and received more than enough to get the job done!

Unfortunately, I didn't always have a lot of time to spend in prayer to make my requests known to God. In fact, the majority of my praying was done on the run. While

I was in the car, at work, making dinner, cleaning the house, and yes, even right in the middle of my conversations! This is what praying without ceasing is all about. It is a habit you develop which causes you to respond automatically to every situation with prayer!

Let's look at other places where Nehemiah automatically responded with prayer. There were many occasions, while working on his assignment, that Nehemiah was attacked. The first being when Sanballat, the enemy of the Jews, verbally insulted the people who were building the wall. The Bible says,

"When Sanballat heard that we were rebuilding the wall, he became angry and greatly incensed. He ridiculed the Jews, and in the presence of his associates and the army of Samaria, he said, 'What are those feeble Jews doing? Will they restore their wall? Will they offer sacrifices? Will they finish in a day? Can they bring the stones back to life from those heaps of rubble - burned as they are?'" (Nehemiah 4:1-2).

The first attack Nehemiah dealt with was verbal. Sanballat insulted the exiles by implying they were too weak and stupid to complete the overwhelming task before them. How did Nehemiah respond to this verbal attack? **The Bible says he instantly prayed.**

"Hear us, O our God, for we are despised. Turn their insults back on their own heads. Give them over as plunder in a land of captivity. Do not cover up their guilt or blot out their sin from Your sight, for they have thrown insults in the face of the builders." (Nehemiah 4:4-5).

Nehemiah's first reaction was to pray. Note that Nehemiah didn't yell or argue with Sanballat. In fact, Nehemiah didn't even get offended, worried or defeated by those words. Instead, Nehemiah prayed and asked God to take care of his enemies for him.

One of the things satan will try to do to stop you from completing your Expected End is verbally attack you. Sanballat's insults were meant to provoke, degrade and discourage the exiles from continuing in their assignment. You see, the enemy uses verbal attacks to get your mind distracted from your project. He knows that, if he can keep you busy thinking about his insults, you won't be able to concentrate on your assignment.

Think about it! How did you respond the last time someone said something bad about you or to you? Did you get mad? Did you go and argue with the person or talk about behind their back? Maybe you didn't say anything, but you let their words hurt you, which then affected your confidence level. Or, perhaps you just replayed the insult repeatedly in your mind, and then spent additional time thinking about what you were going to do in retaliation. The bottom line is this: **If you didn't respond by simply**

praying, the enemy succeeded in keeping your mind distracted from your Expected End.

Nehemiah's sole response to Sanballat's insult was to pray. Nehemiah knew, if he allowed himself and the people to dwell on Sanballat's words, they would be too upset to focus on the wall. What was the result of Nehemiah's prayer? The Bible says,

"So we rebuilt the wall till all of it reached half its height, for the people worked with all their heart" (Nehemiah 4:6). Because Nehemiah prayed and turned it over to God, the exiles stopped thinking about the insults, and then returned to concentrating on their job. In fact, Nehemiah's prayer was so powerful it stirred up the exiles to work *"with all their heart"* in completing their mission!

It is impossible to both pray and think about an insult at the same time! If you don't believe me, try it! When you pray, it takes your mind off the distractions and back onto your mission! Your **first** response to every attack must be prayer, but then you must **continue** praying in order to fully overcome all your situations. Nehemiah **continued** to pray without ceasing throughout the entire time he was working on the wall. Look at this next example.

After Nehemiah prayed against Sanballat's first verbal attack, the exiles were encouraged to return to their work on the wall. Then the Bible says, *"...when Sanballat, Tobiah, the Arabs, the Ammonites and the men of Ashdod heard that the repairs to Jerusalem's walls had gone ahead and that the gaps were being closed, they were very angry. They all plotted together to come and fight against Jerusalem and stir up trouble against it. But we prayed to our God and posted a guard day and night to meet this threat"* (Nehemiah 4:7-9).

Nehemiah's initial prayer strengthened Israel's resolve to complete their mission, but **it also stepped up their enemies resolve to stop it!** As a result, Sanballat and his associates began to stir up even more trouble against Israel! Again, the Scripture shows that Nehemiah's response was, *"we prayed to our God."*

As you pursue your Expected End, you will need to pray **continually.** Nehemiah's enemies didn't stop attacking him after his first prayer, rather their assaults only intensified. Your enemy is not going to stop attacking you after your first, second, or even third prayer. **In fact, the attacks will only get worse just because you are praying.** Remember that prayer prospers you toward your Expected End. (Reread Chapter Nine of this study.) It is why you must continue praying, no matter what!

On what other occasions did Nehemiah use prayer to assist him in completing his assignment? When he felt weak and afraid! The Bible says Nehemiah and the exiles were almost finished with the wall when Sanballat and his associates tried to take Nehemiah's life. The Bible says,

"When word came to Sanballat, Tobiah, Geshem the Arab and the rest of our enemies that I had rebuilt the wall and not a gap was left in it - though up to that time I had not set the doors in the gates - Sanballat and Geshem sent me this message: 'Come, let us meet together in one of the villages on the plain of Ono.' But they were scheming to harm me; so I sent messengers to them with this reply: 'I am carrying on a great project and cannot go down. Why should this work stop while I leave it and go down to you?' Four times they sent me the same message, and each time I gave them the same answer" (Nehemiah 6:1-4).

Nehemiah's enemies, desperate to stop him from completing the wall, were trying to get him in the position where they could physically harm him. Fortunately, because Nehemiah repeatedly refused to meet with them, they could not carry out their scheme. Finally, in an attempt to frighten Nehemiah into complying with their demands, Sanballat sent him this message,

"...It is reported among the neighboring nations... that you and the Jews plan to rebel; therefore you are building the wall, that you may be their king, according to the report. Also you have set up prophets to announce concerning you in Jerusalem, There is a king in Judah. And now this will be reported to the [Persian] king. So, come now and let us take counsel together" (Nehemiah 6:6-7 AMP).

Now, Sanballat was threatening to tell King Artaxerxes that Nehemiah was going to rebel against him. This accusation, if believed, could stop Nehemiah's mission dead in its tracks!

Remember that a similar tactic was used against the first wave of exiles to get them to stop building. Fortunately, though, Nehemiah realized Sanballat's threat was just an attempt to frighten and wear him down to the point where he would quit working on his assignment. Nehemiah replied back to Sanballat, *"...'nothing like what you are saying is happening; you are just making it up out of your head.' They were all trying to frighten us, thinking, 'Their hands will get too weak for the work, and it will not be completed.'* **But I prayed, 'Now strengthen my hands'"** (Nehemiah 6:8-9).

Nehemiah was aware of his enemy's true intentions. This awareness, unfortunately, didn't stop him from being frightened. Nehemiah was also weak from the numerous assaults released on him. But instead of letting those attacks force him to quit, he prayed for the strength he would need to finish the job!

While you are working on your Expected End, the enemy will threaten you, try to frighten you, and even launch physical assaults against you. Through it all, you need to be aware of the true purpose of those attacks. Look again at what Nehemiah said in the Scripture above. *"They were all trying to frighten us, thinking,* **'Their hands will get too weak for the work, and it will not be completed.'"**

The enemy is out to weaken you to the point where you will want to quit. His objective is to beat you down, wear you out and make you too tired to go on. This is why you must be praying! When Nehemiah was worn down, he prayed for strength to finish the job. You will also need to rely on prayer to get the strength you need to complete your mission.

I was so sick the last 12 months I worked on this book. Numerous physical attacks were launched against me. It seemed the closer I got to complete my assignment, the more severe those attacks became. I got the flu half a dozen times in an eight-month period. I developed a severe case of vertigo (this is when you feel like you're spinning out of control even though you are sitting totally still). It lasted a very long four months. Then I was diagnosed with Lupus, a totally debilitating disease where the body literally attacks and destroys itself! Once, I even got violently ill from some vitamins I took! This is when I knew the devil slipped up by being too obvious!

There were days when I was so sick I could barely work on the book. Fortunately, I knew my illnesses were just the enemy's attempts to weaken me to the point where I could not complete my Expected End. So, instead of letting myself quit, I prayed for strength. Sometimes, I would be so physically overwhelmed all I could pray was the word "help" repeatedly in my mind. Fortunately, because I responded with this simple prayer, I was supernaturally enabled to finish my assignment.

Many times Nehemiah's enemies used fear and the threat of physical harm to try to get him to stop working on the wall (Nehemiah 6:10-14). Fortunately, Nehemiah continuously responded to each attack with prayer, and because he did, the Scripture says, "...the wall was completed... in fifty-two days" (Nehemiah 6:15).

While you are pursuing your assignment, you will need to pray without ceasing. The way you do this is simple. Just remind yourself to pray about every part of your day. As you do, you will eventually form the habit where you naturally respond to all your situations with prayer. Remember that your prayers don't need to be long and religious-sounding. They can be given in an instant, even in between breaths, like Nehemiah when he was speaking to the king. The point being, if you develop a habit of responding to everything with prayer first, you will cultivate a powerful weapon in helping you complete your assignment.

Nehemiah's Reliance on God through Faith and Action

Nehemiah was a great man of prayer, but what other techniques did he utilize to complete his assignment so quickly? From the beginning, Nehemiah used **faith** and **action** to help him finish his mission. Let's look at specific examples.

We will start by going back to where Nehemiah and the exiles were first building the wall. The Scripture says,

"But when Sanballat the Horonite, Tobiah the Ammonite official and Geshem the Arab heard about it, they mocked and ridiculed us. 'What is this you are doing?' they asked. 'Are you rebelling against the king?'" (Nehemiah 2:19).

Again, Nehemiah's enemies were verbally assaulting him. How did Nehemiah react this time? With his faith! Nehemiah 2:20 says, *"I answered them by saying, **'The God of heaven will give us success...'"***

What is so special about this statement? It's what Nehemiah based his whole mission on - his faith in God! Let me explain. Do you remember Psalm 33:10-11?

"The LORD foils the plans of the nations; He thwarts the purposes of the peoples. But the plans of the LORD stand firm forever, the purposes of His heart through all generations."

According to Scripture, any plans you make will fail; but when the Lord gives you a plan, you will always succeed! Nehemiah knew this, which is why he could so boldly say that God, Himself would ensure his success. You see, God planted the idea of rebuilding the wall in Nehemiah's heart. Look at what the Bible records Nehemiah as saying when he first arrived in Jerusalem to secretly inspect the wall.

*"I went to Jerusalem, and after staying there three days I set out during the night with a few men. I had not told anyone what **my God had put in my heart to do for Jerusalem**..."* (Nehemiah 2:11-12).

God gave Nehemiah the idea to rebuild the wall. It was the revelation of his Expected End! That is why Nehemiah could so boldly say God would ensure his success. Rebuilding the wall was God's plan, so nothing in the universe could stop it! However, a failure on the part of Nehemiah and the exiles could exclude them from being a part of it. Nehemiah understood this completely. In fact, it is what he based his faith on!

Once you believe God is absolutely able to ensure the success of your project, you must combine your belief with action, by continuing to do your part to complete the assignment. **Faith** has to be combined with **action.** Here is an example:

When the adversaries of Judah threatened to kill the exiles in order to stop their work, Nehemiah, based on his **faith,** took **action** by arming the people with weapons and stationing them at the lowest parts of the wall. Then Nehemiah commanded the people to have **faith** and take **action** themselves. He said, *"...Don't be afraid of them. Remember the Lord, Who is great and awesome, and fight for your brothers, your sons and your daughters, your wives and your homes"* (Nehemiah 4:14).

Nehemiah gave two instructions to the exiles. First he said, *"Remember the Lord Who is great and awesome," In* other words, have faith in the Lord's ability to complete His plan. Then Nehemiah said, *"...fight for your brothers, your sons and your daughters, your wives and your homes."* Meaning, take action on your faith by doing your part to fight to complete the assignment! So, what happened when Nehemiah told his people to have faith and take action?

"When our enemies heard that we were aware of their plot and that God had frustrated it, we all returned to the wall, each to his own work" (Nehemiah 4:15).

God frustrated the plans of the enemy! Then the exiles were encouraged to continue working on their Expected End!

While I was writing this book, I dealt with many kinds of attacks. Through them all, I continually reminded myself that God told me to write this book. I knew it was His plan, not my own, so nothing would be able to stop it! So, when I was attacked, I would respond by first speaking out my **faith.** Then, I would take **action** by continuing to work on my assignment.

Let me give you some examples of the faith statements I would use to fight my battles. Whenever I was attacked I would say things like:

"God instructed me to write this book. Since He ordered it, nothing can stop me!" Or I would say,

"It wasn't my idea to write this book; it was the Lord's, so He will ensure my success." I would also say, "God said this book will be in every prison in America and across the world!"

The reason why these statements of faith were so important was that they showed I believed God was the Maker of my plan, and therefore its success was ensured!

While you are working to complete your Expected End remember this verse, *"...The plans of the LORD stand firm forever..."* Keep it in front of you at all times. Believe that as long as you are following God's plan and doing your part, the gates of hell will not be able to prevail against you! (Matthew 16:18 KJV)

That brings me to my next point. You are going to need to learn how to fight **while** you continue to take action on your assignment. As I said before, the enemy will launch many attacks against you while you are building, in an effort to get you to quit. During those times, you will need to continue working on your assignment **while** you fight those assaults. The enemy will not stop to take a break just because you are busy. Rather, he will increase the intensity of his attacks because you are continuing to pursue your mission! This is why you will need to learn how to work and fight **at the same time!**

When the Israelites were right in the middle of their building project their enemies threatened to kill them. This is why Nehemiah armed the people with weapons. The Bible says, he instructed the exiles to hold their bows and swords **while they continued to build the wall.**

"...Those who carried materials did their work with one hand and held a weapon in the other, and each of the builders wore his sword at his side as he worked..." (Nehemiah 4:17-18).

Nehemiah made sure the exiles didn't stop working in order to fight the battle. In fact, they continued building while carrying their weapons at the same time!

Let me tell you something. The assaults launched against me while I attempted to finish this book never ceased. If I had stopped working in order to fight them, I would never have finished my assignment! Thankfully, I followed Nehemiah's example and worked, *"with one hand and held a weapon in the other."* However, doing so wasn't always easy.

About eight months before I finished the book, I sent my manuscript to two of my close friends. These were women who were involved in ministries and whom I trusted. Well, months later I received letters back from them that literally knocked the wind out of me.

Along with many other comments, one friend said that I needed to be careful concerning the revelations I wrote in the book. She felt satan had deceived me by disguising himself as an angel of light. The other said the "prosperity" message I taught (the prosperity that comes to those who are pursuing God's assignment) was really just a form of godliness using God and Christianity as a means for gain. These comments, coming from people I really trusted, made a deep, negative impact on me. The whole situation severely hampered my ability to continue working on this book.

At the time I received those letters, I was already extremely weak from my repeated illnesses. I was walking around in a fog from constant flu and fever. I was physically exhausted. I couldn't even move my head without spinning from the vertigo. Plus, I ached everywhere from the Lupus attacking my body. Now, satan was pounding away at my mind, insinuating all my doctrine in the book was total error and offensive to God. Well, the attacks took their toll. I began questioning the validity of the entire study. I even stopped working on it, **which is exactly what the devil wanted!**

Remember that the most powerful weapon in the universe against the kingdom of darkness is the person who is pursuing their God-given purpose. This is why satan was out to make sure *The Captivity Series* would never be finished. Not only is this book my Expected End, but it will also enable thousands of others to claim theirs!!!

When I first received those letters, I abandoned my mission. I let myself be totally overwhelmed for a while. Then, I fasted and sought God to see if what I was being told was true. Thankfully, at the end of the fast, the Lord gave me some powerful Scriptures to assure me that I was on the right track. After this, I took those same Scriptures and used them to fight against the devil's attacks. Plus, I made myself work on the book every day, no matter how I felt. As I fought with my sword in one hand (your sword is the Word) and continued to write with the other, satan backed off because he realized I wasn't going to quit.

Don't let anything distract you from completing your assignment! Do you remember when Nehemiah's adversaries were trying to kill him? Jerusalem's wall was almost done, but the gates and the doors were not set up yet. This is why Nehemiah's enemies were trying to do him in. They wanted to stop him before he could complete the project. Let's review Nehemiah 6:2-3 again,

*"Sanballat and Geshem sent me this message: 'Come, let us meet together in one of the villages on the plain of Ono.' But they were scheming to harm me; so I sent messengers to them with this reply: 'I am carrying on a great project and cannot go down. **Why should the work stop while I leave it and go down to you?'"***

Nehemiah recognized the reason for the attack was to get him to stop working on the wall. This is why he refused to respond to the invitation. You must do the same. Don't ever take time out from your mission to go down to argue with your attackers. Refuse to be distracted from your work. The Bible says Nehemiah's enemies **repeatedly** asked him to meet with them, but he **repeatedly** declined.

*"They sent to me **four times** this way, and **I answered them as before"** (Nehemiah 6:4 AMP). Over and over, the enemy tried to get Nehemiah to stop what he was doing, but Nehemiah repeatedly chose to ignore them and continue his work. When the enemy repeatedly gives you an invitation to engage him, decline his offers. Keep your focus on your mission!

I advise you to read the entire book of Nehemiah, study his tactics and then, more importantly, put them into practice. Learn to pray without ceasing. Always speak out your faith. Take action by continuing to pursue your assignment. Remember to fight with one hand, while you work with the other. Don't let anything cause you to quit! These techniques will greatly assist you in handling the multitude of attacks you will face as you work toward completing your Expected End. If you put them into practice, you will succeed and step into your inheritance.

Lesson Twenty-Three

1. Nehemiah learned to *"pray without ceasing."* What do you think that means?

2. Nehemiah responded to every attack he faced with P _____, F _____ , and A _____.

3. Write Psalm 33:10-11 in the space below. Describe what this verse has to do with succeeding in your Expected End.

4. Write down a statement of faith you can say aloud or in prayer when you are attacked while pursuing your Expected End.

5. What does the following verse mean when it comes to completing your Expected End? *"...Those who carried materials did their work with one hand and held a weapon in the other, and each of the builders wore his sword at his side as he worked..."* (Nehemiah 4: 17-18).

6. The main goal of the enemy is to get you to stop working on your assignment. No matter how he attacks you, do not quit! Do not let yourself be distracted from your mission. If the enemy tries to distract you, give him the same answer Nehemiah did. Write Nehemiah 6:3 below.

CHAPTER TWENTY-FOUR

WHERE'S THE MONEY, HONEY?

"...The expenses of these men are to be fully paid out of the royal treasury, from the revenues of Trans-Euphrates, so that the work will not stop."
Ezra 6:8

Your money is in your mission. As long as you are pursuing your Expected End, God will make sure you are able to meet all your financial obligations, both Kingdom and personal. Why would the Lord do this? The above Scripture tells us, **"so that the work will not stop."** Let me explain.

God's priority for money is to use it to build His Kingdom. It takes money to spread the Gospel. If you don't have money, you can't print tracts or books. You can't produce television or radio programs. You can't run a church or travel around spreading the good news. This is one reason why God financially prospers His servants, *"so that the work will not stop."* Face it, the guy who said, "Money makes the world go around" wasn't totally incorrect. Money is one of the vehicles God uses to cover the earth with the knowledge of Himself.

Another reason why God financially increases those who are pursuing their Expected End is because it takes time, energy and total commitment on your part to walk out your assignment. If you are in a poor financial position, constantly laboring to pay bills, you won't be able to work on your mission. God providentially provides for His servants who are pursuing their Expected End so they can be freed up to do His work. When God's servants are free to pursue their Kingdom purposes, His *"work will not stop."*

God also uses money just to bless us! When you choose to lay down your life to make God and the building of His Kingdom your first priority, Scripture says He will take care of all your needs. In Matthew 6:31-33, Jesus said,

"...do not worry, saying, 'What shall we eat?' or 'What shall we drink?' or 'What shall we wear?' For the pagans run after all these things, and **your heavenly Father knows that you need them. But seek first His kingdom and His righteousness and all these things will be given to you as well."**

The purpose of your Expected End is to build God's Kingdom. When you choose to make this your first priority, God will give you everything else you need! When you are pursuing your assignment, you work for God. You are His employee, on His payroll. And let me assure you, that you will find, God is the most generous employer in the universe!

It is especially important for all ex-felons to understand the biblical truth that God prospers those who pursue their assignments. Why? Prior to being arrested, many of us resorted to crime in order to get money. God does not want you to be in this position again. **He has a better way for you to earn a living!** In this chapter, I am going to prove through Scripture, that your future prosperity lies in your assignment. Now is your time to make money in a righteous manner. Focus on your Expected End, and have all your needs fulfilled by God.

Every group of exiles who returned to Jerusalem prospered because they were pursuing their Expected End. Zerubbabel and his people prospered because they were on a mission to rebuild the temple. Ezra and his group were given massive wealth because they were on a mission to teach the Word of God and restore temple service. Nehemiah was given all the materials he needed to rebuild Jerusalem's wall, set up its gates and complete his assignment. **Each of the three groups received some kind of financial assistance because they were pursuing their Expected End!** In this chapter, we are going to look at their examples so you can see, beyond a shadow of doubt, that God prospers His people who are pursuing their Kingdom purposes.

In the first chapter of Ezra, God moved the heart of King Cyrus to make a proclamation concerning the first wave of captives returning to Jerusalem. The Bible records Cyrus as saying,

"This is what Cyrus king of Persia says: 'The Lord, the God of heaven, has given me all the kingdoms of the earth and He has appointed me to build a temple for Him at Jerusalem in Judah. Anyone of His people among you- may his God be with him, and let him go up to Jerusalem in Judah and build the temple of the Lord... And the people of any place where survivors may now be living are to **provide him with silver and gold, with goods and livestock, and with freewill offerings for the temple of God** *in Jerusalem'"* (Ezra 1:2-4).

King Cyrus issued an order for every one left in Babylon to provide the returning exiles with money and goods to rebuild the temple in Jerusalem! In response to the kings' proclamation, Ezra 1:6-7 says, *"All their neighbors assisted them with articles of silver and gold, with goods and livestock, and with valuable gifts, in addition to all the freewill offerings. Moreover, King Cyrus brought out the articles belonging to the temple of the LORD, which Nebuchadnezzar had carried away from Jerusalem..."*

Cyrus's order prompted a lot of support. The first group of returnees left Babylon with money, provisions to live on, valuable gifts, freewill offerings, and 5,400 silver and gold vessels for use in the temple. In all, a very substantial amount and more than enough to enable the exiles to walk out their Expected End!

The first group of returning exiles experienced immense prosperity because they were on an assignment. In fact, the only time their prosperity stopped was when they quit working on the temple. Do you remember what happened when the enemies of Israel sent a letter to King Artaxerxes? The king ordered the exiles to stop building. Well, unfortunately they did, which is when their prosperity ceased.

However, when the prophet Haggai told the people to return to their assignment, and they obeyed, their prosperity returned. Later on though, the exiles were attacked again. A second letter of accusation was sent to the new king of Persia, King Darius. This time, the exiles didn't quit working on the temple, but rather **continued to pursue their assignment.** And, because they did, the Scripture says, "*...the eye of their God was upon the elders of the Jews so the enemy could not make them stop...*" (Ezra 5:5 AMP). Check out the amazing reply King Darius sent back to the second letter.

"Now then, Tattenai, governor of Trans-Euphrates, and Shethar-Bozenai and you, their fellow officials of that province, stay away from there. ***Do not interfere with the work on this temple of God. Let the governor of the Jews and the Jewish elders rebuild this house of God on its site.*** *Moreover, I hereby decree what you are to do for these elders of the Jews in the construction of this house of God:* ***The expenses of these men are to be fully paid out of the royal treasury, from the revenues of Trans-Euphrates, so that the work will not stop. Whatever is needed - young bulls, rams, male lambs for burnt offerings to the God of heaven, and wheat, salt, wine and oil, as requested by the priests in Jerusalem - must be given them daily without fail... Furthermore, I decree that if anyone changes this edict, a beam is to be pulled from his house and he is to be lifted up and impaled on it..."* (Ezra 6:6-9, 11).

In response to the letter, King Darius first decreed that the Israelites be allowed to continue building! Then the king told Tattenai and his fellow officials to pay for all the exiles' expenses, plus give them everything they needed to complete the temple! Darius even said anyone who didn't comply with his order would be killed! This is how seriously God takes providing for His servants who are pursuing their purpose! Notice again, though, why God does this,

"The expenses of these men are to be fully paid out of the royal treasury... ***so that the work will not stop."***

God will not allow His work to be stopped. This Scripture proves that He will do whatever is necessary to supernaturally prosper His servants so they can get the job done!

Another example of this comes from the second wave of returnees. When Ezra left Babylon on his mission, he was given a large amount of wealth. The Bible says right before he went to Jerusalem, King Artaxerxes gave him a letter.

"I make a decree that all of the people of Israel and of their priests and Levites in my realm, who offer freely to go up to Jerusalem, may go with you. For you are sent by the

king and his seven counselors to inquire about Judah and Jerusalem according to the instruction of your God... And to carry the silver and gold which the king and his counselors have freely offered to the God of Israel... and all the silver and gold that you may find in all the province of Babylonia, with the freewill offerings of the people and of the priests, offered willingly for the house of their God in Jerusalem... And whatever more shall be needful for the house of your God which you shall have occasion to provide, provide it out of the king's treasury" (Ezra 7:13-16, 20 AMP).

Ezra received all the financial help he needed to carry out his assignment. The king gave silver and gold for use in the house of the Lord. He also told Ezra he could have all the silver and gold he could find in the province of Babylonia. In addition, the king said he would provide from his own treasury anything else Ezra needed.

Then, if this wasn't enough, King Artaxerxes also issued an additional order to his royal treasurers on the Jerusalem side of the Euphrates. He told them to provide Ezra with whatever he needed once he arrived home. Ezra 7:21-23 states,

"Now I, King Artaxerxes, order all the treasurers of Trans-Euphrates to provide with diligence whatever Ezra the priest, a teacher of the Law of the God of heaven, may ask of you - up to a hundred talents of silver, a hundred cors of wheat, a hundred baths of wine, a hundred baths of olive oil, and salt without limit. Whatever the God of heaven has prescribed, let it be done with diligence for the temple of God in heaven..."

In ancient times, a hundred talents of silver weighed the equivalent of 7,500 lbs. A hundred baths were equal to 600 gallons. In Persia, according to biblical historians, salt was only made available to palace royalty; but here, Ezra was given *"salt without limit"* because he was on a mission from God.

Each group of exiles pursuing their Expected End received everything they needed to complete it. You might be wondering, though, if God's generous provision is only for use in your assignment. Well, in King Artaxerxes's letter to Ezra, the king closes by giving Ezra an instruction on how to spend the money he was given. The Bible says,

"Therefore you shall with all speed and exactness buy with this money young bulls, rams, lambs, with their cereal offerings and drink offerings, and then offer them on the altar of the house of your God in Jerusalem. And whatever shall seem good to you and to your brethren to do with the rest of the silver and the gold, that do after the will of your God" (Ezra 7:17-18 AMP).

The king instructed Ezra to **first** spend the money on the supplies he would need to run the temple. Then, the king said, *"And whatever shall seem good to you and to your brethren to do with the rest of the silver and the gold, **that do after the will of your God."*** This Scripture says it all. The first and foremost thing you must do with the provisions you receive is ***"the will of your God"*** and His will must be carried out with "all **speed** and **exactness,**" as the king instructed. However, once you've taken care of the needs of your mission, being a good steward over the money, **completely** doing what God requires, then, *"...whatever shall seem good to you and to your brethren to do with the rest of the silver and the gold, that do..."*

Along with the financial needs of your mission, God is also going to take care of your personal needs. God rewards His people who are committed to His purposes. In Mark 10:29-30, Jesus says,

"I tell you the truth... no one who has left home or brothers or sisters or mother or father or children or fields for me and the gospel will fail to receive a hundred times as much in this present age (homes, brothers, sisters, mothers, children, and fields - and with them, persecutions) and in the age to come, eternal life."

People will argue we shouldn't focus on rewards or what we can get out of working for the Lord. However, God promises you will be rewarded, and a hundred-fold at that. Not only in the age to come, but also *"in this present age"* for the sacrifices you made to pursue your Expected End.

As the Scripture above says, persecutions will come along with your blessings, as we have so clearly seen throughout this study. So, you must be a good steward over all God gives you. The Bible says that to whom much is given, much is required (Luke 12:48). If you do not handle the blessings God bestows on you with the utmost care and integrity, **He will take them away.** In the matter of finances, you will be repeatedly tried and tested by the Father. This is why you must always conduct yourself in a manner worthy of Him.

Every exile who returned home on a mission received all the provisions necessary to complete their assignment. Even Nehemiah was given the beams and timbers he needed to set up Jerusalem's gates. So, if your mission requires ten dollars or a hundred thousand, God will make sure you get it. He will also prosper you for the sacrifices you make to build His Kingdom.

Now, let me share with you the last chapter of this study, the promise of my Expected End!

Lesson Twenty-Four

1. What is God's priority for your finances?

2. As long as you are pursuing your Expected End, God will providentially provide for all your needs, both Kingdom and personal. Why would He do this? (Your answer lies in Ezra 6:8)

3. What would cause God to stop prospering you?

4. Pick one of the three groups of exiles that returned to Jerusalem on a mission. Name the mission they were on and the provisions they received because of their assignment.

5. According to the following Scripture, what is the first and foremost thing you must do with the provisions you receive? *"And whatever shall seem good to you and to your brethren to do with the rest of the silver and the gold, that do after the will of your God."* After you've taken care of the needs of your mission, being a good steward over all you have, and completely doing what God requires, what can you do with the rest of the provisions you receive?

6. The Bible promises that God will bless His people who are pursuing their kingdom assignments. Write down this promise from Mark 10:29-30.

CHAPTER TWENTY-FIVE

My Expected End

"For I know the thoughts that I think toward you, saith the Lord, thoughts of peace, and not of evil, to give you an Expected End."
Jeremiah 29:11 KJV

In January, 2006, I'd been out of prison for almost three years, and was going into my fourth year of writing *The Captivity Series.* Even though I was close to finishing the book, it seemed as if I would never be done. The whole process was taking so long it felt like a pregnancy, years overdue. Inside of me was a huge baby, kicking hard at my rib cage, wanting out!

A year earlier in 2005, I'd fought battles so fierce there were moments when it looked like I was a goner. That entire year, I was assaulted mentally, spiritually and emotionally at every corner. Then, I was diagnosed with Lupus, a disease where the body literally attacks and destroys itself. Just when I thought I might actually die, the Lord came to my rescue by supernaturally healing me!! When it happened, I knew in my spirit that the Lord made me well so I could complete my mission. Once I was healed, I thought all the fighting was over. How mistaken I was.

Now, 2006, brought on a completely new war, which was so fierce; it made me feel like I was being repeatedly run over by a tank. Satan found the chink in my armor, my beloved husband; and he was unleashing the very forces of hell against our marriage. Since my husband and I were partners in the mission, the devil knew if he could shipwreck us, he could keep the assignment from being completed. So day after day, Bobby and I were under attack until finally we teetered on the brink of total destruction. Until then, I was confident nothing could make me go down for the count. However, though my husband and I were not physically battling each other, it seemed like I was fighting in a heavyweight bout. It was the 13th round, I was tired and the mat was looking very inviting. Yet through it all, the excitement of what was growing in my belly gave me the power to continue. Figuratively speaking, I was very anxious for that rapidly approaching moment, when my water would break, and I would go into labor to produce something fantastic, and well worth the wait!

One Sunday night in mid February, I was sitting in front of the computer, struggling. I was desperately trying to peck out some kind of progress on the book when my phone rang. Since I never took calls on Sunday, I surprised myself when suddenly I reached over to answer it. "This is Katie," I said, wondering why I just broke my rule.

"Hi Katie, it's Stephanie Medeiros!" I heard her say. "How are you doing?"

"Hey, girl! I'm doing ok," I replied to her greeting. "The question is, 'How are you?'" I continued. I couldn't help but wonder why Stephanie was calling me since we barely knew each other. Though we met the previous year at my accountant's office, we didn't get a chance to develop our friendship because she left after becoming very ill. When I asked her how she was doing, I heard her take a huge deep breath before proceeding to tell me how grave her situation was.

"Well, the doctors are giving me 18 months to live." She said in a flat tone.

This news came as a shock as I knew Stephanie was very sick but had no idea she was so near death. Surprisingly though, she sounded good, and didn't seem to want to focus our discussion on her problem. In fact, after telling me just a few more details she suddenly changed the subject.

"Anyway," she said, as she quickly shifted gears. "Let me tell you the real reason why I called."

"Ok," I responded, now wondering what was really going on.

"Well, even though I am not supposed to leave the house, I decided I needed to get out," she started, "so, I went to a Joyce Meyer seminar this weekend. Do you know who she is?"

At this, my first thought was, "Who didn't?" After all, Joyce Meyer was seen every day on television by almost two-thirds of the world. Stephanie though, was obviously unaware of this, so I casually responded with, "Sure I do," as to not take away from her thunder.

"Well, I didn't know who she was until just lately." Stephanie continued, "But, when I went to her seminar, I had a fantastic time!"

As Stephanie proceeded to give me the recap of everything she heard in the conference, I could feel her enthusiasm build. By the end of her detailed description, she was really excited, but then a few seconds later I found out the real reason why she was so wound up. She was about to throw me a pitch.

"While I was there," Stephanie said, finally getting to the bottom line, "I felt like there was something important I was supposed to do, but I didn't know what it was." "Well, this morning," she continued, "I saw Joyce on television talking about her prison ministry, then suddenly I knew" At this statement, Stephanie paused ever so slightly before letting it fly.

"I am supposed to tell you to take your book to Joyce while she is in town," she said. "Really?" I replied sharply, trying to dodge her fastball as it whirled at me. "Yes. Definitely." she replied back, with a total air of assurance.

Inside I laughed. Stephanie's confidence, I thought, was rather bold; especially considering she had never read my book! For all she knew, it was total junk, a factor that at the moment didn't seem to bother her at all.

"But it's too late," I replied. "The conference is over."

At this, Stephanie quickly interjected with, "Yes, but Joyce is having a book signing in town this Thursday."

This was a fact I already knew. As a partner with Joyce Meyer Ministries, I received her monthly newsletter with the announcements of all her upcoming events. Though Stephanie didn't know it, I already considered going to the book signing, but decided against it. The reason being, I already asked God if I should go, and He said nothing. Therefore, I was sure I wasn't to attend.

Stephanie, however, was quite sure of the opposite. "Listen," she said insistently, "I know, I heard from the Lord! Plus," she continued, with her voice intensifying, "when I went to call you, I found your phone number right on top of my desk, which if you saw my desk, you would know is a complete miracle!"

At this comment, I remembered that I answered my phone on a Sunday, which also never happened.

"Ok, I'll tell you what," I said conceding to her. "I will pray, and ask God myself if I should go. Then I will call you back to let you know what He says, ok?"

"Good," she said firmly, like to a child who finally decided to obey.

"In the meantime," I continued, ignoring her motherly impulses. "I'm going to email you my book, so you can read it."

"Alright," she said casually, sounding as though it wouldn't make any difference whether she read it or not.

"Then, after you read it," I said with a lot of emphasis. "You can let me know if you still feel the same."

She agreed, confirming her email address before hanging up. Then, after pausing a minute to review our conversation, I thought to myself in amazement,

"Out of all the people in the world, I can't believe she told me to take my book to Joyce Meyer!" The reason I was so stunned, was that Stephanie had absolutely no idea what God had told me about Joyce four years earlier...

I was still in prison at the time, just beginning to write the book. One day, while in the shower, I asked the Lord how I was going to possibly get my book to the millions of prisoners who needed it. After all, it wasn't like I could just pass around the collection plate. They didn't have any money, and neither did I. As I stood underneath the hot water pouring out of the headless shower pipe, I suddenly thought of Joyce Meyer. Many inmates received her books, including myself. Her ministry sent thousands of books into prisons across the world.

"I could do anything with the help of a ministry like hers." I thought wistfully.

As I massaged a palm-full of cheap Suave conditioner into my hair, I let my mind wander away. Almost instantly, I saw myself standing in front of a large crowd talking about one of Joyce's books. This off-the-cuff "daydream" continued for some time, until I finally made myself snap out of it.

"That was strange," I thought. "Why would I see myself promoting someone else's book?"

As I pondered this odd vision, while rinsing the conditioner from my hair, I suddenly got an urgent feeling God wanted to speak to me. So, I turned the water off, and started to dry, all the while thinking about Joyce's ministry. Was I just daydreaming, or was God trying to tell me something? Suddenly, I couldn't wait to find out, so I threw on my sweats, even though I was still damp, then high-tailed it to my cell.

When I walked in, both my roommates were engrossed in their own reading. Thankful, I quickly put away my shower bag, and threw myself down on the bunk with my Bible. As soon as I turned to my daily reading in Galatians, the Lord turned on the juice. The very first thing I read was Paul saying this:

"I want you to know, brothers, that the gospel I preached is not something that man made up. I did not receive it from any man, nor was I taught it; rather I received it by revelation from Jesus Christ" (Galatians 1:11-12).

Right away, I knew God was talking about *The Captivity Series.* Just like Paul, the revelations I was receiving were not my own, but God's. So, in the verses following, where Paul wrote of how God enabled him to spread his message across the entire ancient world, I knew the Lord was also about to tell me how He would spread *The Captivity Series* across the entire prison system.

In Galatians, the Lord had divinely instructed Paul to go to Jerusalem to meet with Peter, James and John, the original apostles of Jesus. Paul took his gospel to these men to see if they agreed with it. At that time, the apostles were the leaders of the entire Christian church, so they were the ones who could give Paul the support he needed to spread his teachings. The problem was that Peter, James and John had spent time with Jesus while He was on earth, whereas Paul had not. So, he was considered a nobody compared to them. Paul even said he was, *"personally unknown to the churches of Judea that are in Christ"* (Galatians 1:22). So, why would anyone take his message seriously?

Right then, I knew God was talking to me. I was just like Paul, a nobody, a lowly convict. So, why would anyone want to take my message seriously? None of the leaders of the big ministries knew me, but like the apostles were to Paul, those leaders were the ones who could enable me to fully carry out my mission.

As I paused to dwell on this stark reality, all the impossibilities began to swarm my head like angry bees. I was a felon with a violent past. If I came knocking at Joyce Meyer's door, I probably wouldn't get any further than the lobby, or be told to get in line behind the millions of people who were in front of me. Even if I did get in, would anyone take the time to hear my message, not to mention give me the massive support I needed to fulfill my mission?

To even, believe, I could receive help from someone like Joyce Meyer was not only farfetched, but seemed totally impossible. As I let this thought start to take over my brain, I suddenly realized what I was doing: I was daring to put a limit on God! Instantly convicted, I knew I needed to immediately stop entertaining all dream-killer thoughts and return to Scripture to see what the Lord wanted to say. Sure enough, when I went back to see what happened to Paul, everything dramatically changed!

In the next verses, Paul addressed the very thing I was so concerned about. He said,

"As for those who seemed to be important—whatever they were makes no difference to me; God does not judge by external appearance—those men added nothing to my message. On the contrary, they saw that I had been entrusted with the task of preaching the gospel to the Gentiles, just as Peter had been to the Jews" (Galatians 2:6-7).

I was awestruck! In one sentence, Paul put it all in perspective. He said it didn't matter that he was not a person of great importance. The Lord was in charge of making a way for him. In fact, when Paul presented his revelations to the apostles, they recognized he was entrusted by God to carry out his mission!

As I read the verse over, I thought I heard God whisper into my spirit, "They will recognize the same thing about you." Would they? Would God move the hearts of the "big shots" of the church, so I could proclaim my gospel around the world? I needed to know.

Now, I felt urgency in my reading. Though the apostles saw Paul was entrusted to preach the Gospel, did they actually help him pursue His mission? I dug into the next verses as if my very existence depended on them. Would God confirm what I believed He was telling me, or would I find out that I was just daydreaming after all? I took a deep breath, and held it as I read on. Thankfully, I only had to go a few more lines before I saw I wasn't going to be disappointed. When I reached the answer I was hoping for, I was so relieved that I let out a loud "whoosh" of air. Paul said,

"And when they knew (perceived, recognized, understood, and acknowledged) the grace (God's unmerited favor and spiritual blessing) that had been bestowed upon me, **James and Cephas (Peter) and John, who were reputed to be pillars of the Jerusalem church, gave to me and Barnabas the right hand of fellowship** *with the understanding that we should go to the Gentiles and they to the circumcised (Jews)"* (Galatians 2:9 AMP).

Whoa! The power of God came over me, and I trembled as I read it. It was the answer to my question. Peter, James and John, the reputed pillars of the Jerusalem church, gave Paul all the help he needed to fulfill his mission! The reality of what this meant to me was almost too incredible to comprehend. God was actually saying He was going to give me, a total nobody, a lowly convict, favor with one of the biggest ministries in the world! Like the high apostles, who gave Paul the right hand of fellowship, Joyce Meyer Ministries would help me. At this thought, a feeling of inexpressible elation surrounded me, like a soothing bath of warm water. It felt so good; I wanted to soak in it forever.

So now, here it was four years later, and a woman I barely knew was telling me to take my book to Joyce. Coincidence? I didn't believe in it. However, I already asked God if I should go to the book signing, and He said nothing. So, what was really going on? The only way to find out was to ask again. So, I immediately went to God in prayer.

"Lord, I already asked you this, and you said nothing," I began. "So, I think the answer is no, but I just wanted to double check." Then, I paused briefly, as to get quiet enough to hear Him, before calmly saying, "Am I supposed to go to the book signing?"

Not even a fraction of a second passed when I heard in my mind, "Galatians 2:9." Since I couldn't remember exactly what verse this was, I flipped open my Bible to Galatians, then almost fainted when I read it.

"...James and Cephas (Peter) and John, who were reputed to be pillars of the Jerusalem church, **gave to me and Barnabas the right hand of fellowship..."**

"Oh my!" I thought, my stomach muscles convulsing. **"This is it, the promise I've been waiting for!"** I was supposed to go. The time was finally here, and I literally felt sick to my stomach! How could I possibly give my little book to a woman like Joyce Meyer? It wasn't even finished, and the book signing was just four days away! There was no way I could be ready by then.

I panicked. My mind did zero-to-sixty in one minute. I went from rehearsing what I would say to Joyce, to trying to figure out how to get out of going! Then, in the middle of my freak out, God put on the brakes by reminding me of who was in charge. He was, and His timing was always perfect. He had given Paul a divine revelation to take his message to the apostles. And, well, this was my revelation! I was to go, whether I felt ready or not, because God would take care of the rest. So, I called Stephanie, and simply said, "We're going!"

The book signing was Thursday, which meant I had three days to get the manuscript in order. Using every free minute of my time to get prepared, it took me to the very last minute to finish up. Finally, at 9 p.m. on Wednesday night, I was at the printer's office making copies. I was as ready as I could be.

Thursday morning arrived, and even though Stephanie thought she couldn't make it, she came anyway with an IV line going to her heart, hidden in the sleeve of her blouse. On the way to the book signing, we talked about her situation.

"God is going to heal me," she began. "I really believe it."

Unfortunately, the look on her face told me a completely different story. Her expression was clouded with doubt, and I could tell she didn't really believe it at all.

As I looked at this woman who was driving me to my date with destiny, I thought to myself, "If there was a room full of people, I would have never picked her."

We were total opposites. She was a corporate executive, suits and all. I lived in my jeans, and didn't know what the word "networking" meant. She was the kind of woman who would run the church's scrap booking ministry, whereas I just liked to scrap. She was such a goodie-two-shoes; she would give Mary Poppins a run for her money. As for me, well…

Stephanie, however, was obviously God's perfect choice. Just by her being here, He was making it clear that she was involved in the mission. As the importance of this revelation hit me, I felt a quickening in my spirit for her, and I turned so I could look her dead in the eye.

"One thing I know for sure," I said, the preacher rising up in me. "God heals His people who are pursuing their created purpose." Then, in response to her doubt, I finished with, "You are now a part of this mission, so He is going to make sure you are well enough to carry it out!"

At this, Stephanie gave me a funny little look, which said, "Hey, I'm just giving you a ride to the bookstore!"

When we arrived at the bookstore, the place was packed, with not a parking spot in sight. Then, right as we pulled up, a man backed his car out of a space, only 20-feet away from the front of the building. Delighted, Stephanie and I looked at each other wide eyed. It was the first sign we were in the right place at the right time.

We walked in, were assigned a number for our group, and then went to look at some of Joyce's books. After we picked out a couple, Stephanie suggested we pray. So, we went to the coffee bar to look for a place to sit, but there were no tables, and lots of people were standing around waiting.

Suddenly, a man approached us, out of all the people standing there, to ask if we wanted his table. Looking over, I saw it was in a private corner away from everyone else, the perfect place to pray. Once again, Stephanie and I looked at each other with a knowing look.

After gratefully accepting the offer, we prayed, drank some coffee, and then went to pay for our books. Just as I was signing the credit card receipt, they called our number. Everything was going like clockwork. When we went to stand in line, we immediately struck up a conversation with two women next to us. We were only talking with them for a few minutes when one of the women named Sandy looked at Stephanie, and said,

"You are ill." Then, accentuating her statement she said again, "No, you are very ill. May I pray for you?"

Stephanie began to weep. Neither one of us had said a word about her illness. Even Stephanie's IV line couldn't have given her away, as it was hidden. However, the Holy Spirit was obviously leading Sandy as she proceeded to place her hands right on the source of Stephanie's infection! Instantly, I felt a wave of power hit me, even though I was standing three feet away! When I looked at Stephanie, she was sweating and turning bright red.

As the line moved forward, we all moved with it, with Sandy silently praying over my new friend the entire time. Then, right when we came to the end of the line, she finished her prayer, and I turned to see we were next to meet with Joyce!

As I walked up to the table, I was so nervous, I began feeling queasy. Joyce was sitting with her husband Dave, and two of their children who worked for the ministry. When it came time for me to hand her my book, everything got fuzzy. Stephanie later on told me that I said a million things in less than a minute without sounding hurried. She also said Dave Meyer was watching me the whole time, focused in on my every word. When I turned to leave, he reached out his right hand, and shook mine, while looking me square in the eye. It wasn't until I walked away that I realized he had literally given me the "right hand of fellowship!"

Later on after the book signing, Stephanie went home, and a nurse came to her house to draw blood. Stephanie's previous blood test had showed her white cell count was dangerously elevated, so a new treatment of IV antibiotics was scheduled to start the very next day. Unfortunately, with the treatment came a very serious side effect. It would cause Stephanie to go completely deaf.

Two weeks later her doctor called.

"We are going to stop the treatment," the doctor said matter-of-factly. "Why?" Stephanie responded with total surprise.

"Because there is nothing wrong with you now." The doctor continued, "We received your blood work back from two weeks ago, and it was perfectly normal."

The results the doctor was referring to were from the blood test taken right after the book signing. Results the doctor could not explain. Stephanie had been supernaturally healed!

Two weeks later while at a church service together, Stephanie received a revelation. In the middle of the service she looked over at me, with tears rolling down her face, and said, "God just told me He healed me for you."

When she said that, the power of the Spirit came upon me, and I wept. I knew what the Lord meant. He made her well so she could help me complete the mission!

And help me she did. Until then, I was alone in the project. Now, I had assistance. Stephanie and I were complete opposites, but because she possessed all the skills I lacked, the two of us combined, became a powerful force. Doors, which were never opened to me previously now, swung wide; as Stephanie went before me with such power, it was as if the words, *"show me favor,"* were tattooed on her forehead! A cover was designed for the book, a website was made, and books were printed and sent out. Even though we started in only three prisons, the book was soon in almost a hundred facilities across the country.

Then something happened. I came home one day, and walked out to the postbox to pick up the mail. It contained the usual assortment of bills and credit card offers. Fortunately though, the pitiful pile was redeemed by the arrival of my monthly Joyce Meyer newsletter. As I strolled back into the house, I swooped up our cat, George, who was loudly demanding food, then set down the mail on the breakfast bar so I could feed his hungry face.

After tossing the empty cat food can into the trash, I grabbed Joyce's newsletter, then sat down on the couch to give it a look. When I turned over the envelope, I noticed the flap was open. The letter was unsealed. Thankful that its contents were still inside, I pulled it out, and began to read. Immediately though, I noticed it didn't look like any newsletter I'd ever received before. In fact, it was totally different. This is when my eyes began to scan the page. Words like "Dear Katie" and "manuscript" jumped out at me. It was then I recognized that, indeed, it wasn't what I first thought. In fact, it was a personal letter to me from Joyce Meyer herself!

Everything got totally blurry for a second. I fought the panic now rising fast inside of me. I struggled to calm down, without success, trying to get my vision to clear, so I could read. Yes, read the personal letter I was holding in my hands from a woman whose ministry covered two thirds of the world! A woman whom God Himself promised would give me the right hand of fellowship! A woman whose ministry could enable my ministry to help thousands, even millions of people!

I took a deep breath in order to stop myself from hyper-ventilating, then quickly poured over the letter that could forever change my destiny....

TO THE READER OF THIS STUDY

Right now, I am living out this final chapter! In these next years, the Lord said He would do the IMPOSSIBLE for this ministry! I can't wait to share with you the fulfillment of this promise! As we wait for these events to come to pass, let me say this:

The mission of Expected End Ministries is to get *The Captivity Series* into the hands of every prisoner in America and beyond. If you share in this vision and you feel a burning in your spirit right now, you are one of the people God has chosen to help! The current needs of this ministry are:

- Prayer Partners.

- Donations for the cost of publishing which enable Expected End Ministries to reach more prisons, jails, detention centers, halfway houses, rehabilitation centers, and juvenile detention centers.*

- Monthly partners to help with the cost of running this ministry.*

  * All donations are tax-deductible.

When Ezekiel prophesied in the valley of dry bones, those bones represented the Israelite captives who were in Babylon in a dry, spiritless state. There are multitudes of people in prison today in the same condition. Prisoners who are like dry bones because they lack their true created purpose.

You, together with Expected End Ministries, have the opportunity to help them find their Expected End through the vehicle of *The Captivity Series.* We believe this study will cause the captives to stand up on their feet and become *"A VAST ARMY"* (Ezekiel 37:10), for the Kingdom of God!

Thank you for your support, and may the Lord bless you,

Katie Souza and the staff of Expected End Ministries

PRISONS HOLD GOD'S TREASURES

by Bill Yount

It was late and I was tired, wanting to go to sleep, but God wanted to talk; it was about midnight, but it dawned on me that God does not sleep. His question made me restless. "Bill, where on earth does man keep his most priceless treasures and valuables?" I said, "Lord, usually these treasures like gold, silver, diamonds and precious jewels are kept locked up somewhere out of sight, usually with guards and security to keep them under lock and key." God spoke, "Like man, My most valuable treasures on earth are also locked up." I then saw Jesus standing in front of seemingly thousands of prisons and jails. The Lord said, "These have almost been destroyed by the enemy, but these ones have the greatest potential to be used and to bring forth glory to My name. Tell My people, I am going this hour to the prisons to activate the gifts and callings that lie dormant in these lives that were given before the foundation of the earth. Out from these walls will come forth an Army of Spirituals, who will have power to literally kick down the gates of hell and overcome satanic powers that are holding many of My own people bound in My own house.

Tell My people that great treasure is behind these walls, in these forgotten vessels. My people must come forth and touch these ones, for a mighty anointing will be unleashed upon these for future victory in My Kingdom. THEY MUST BE RESTORED."

I then saw the Lord step up to the prison doors with a key. One key fit every lock and the gates began to open. I then heard and saw great explosions, which sounded like dynamite going off behind the walls. It sounded like all-out spiritual warfare. Jesus turned and said, "Tell My people to go in now and pick up the spoil and rescue these." Jesus then began walking in and touching inmates who were thronging Him. Many being touched instantly began to have a golden glow come over them. God spoke to me, "THERE'S THE GOLD!" Others had a silver glow around them. God said, "THERE'S THE SILVER!"

Like slow motion they began to grow into what appeared to be giant knights in armor-like warriors. They had on the entire armor of God and every piece was solid and pure gold! Even golden shields! When I saw the golden shields, I heard God say to these warriors: "Now go and take what satan has taught you and use it against him. Go and pull down the strongholds coming against MY church." The spiritual giants then started stepping over the prison walls with no one to resist them, and they went immediately to the very front line of the battle with the enemy. I saw them walk right past the church; and big-name ministers known for their power with God were surpassed by the giant warriors, like David going after Goliath! They crossed the enemy's line and started delivering many of God's people from the clutches of satan while demons trembled and fled out of sight at their presence. No one, not even the church, seemed to know who these spiritual giants were or where they came from. All you could see was the armor, the golden armor of God, from head to foot, and the shields of gold were there. The shields were restored to God's House and there was great victory and rejoicing.

I also saw silver, precious treasures, and vessels being brought in. Beneath the gold and silver were the people that nobody knew: REJECTS OF SOCIETY, STREET PEOPLE, THE OUT-CASTS, THE POOR and the DESPISED. These were the treasures that were missing from His House.

In closing, the Lord said, "If My people want to know where they are needed, tell them they are needed in the STREETS, the HOSPITALS, the MISSIONS, and PRISONS. When they come there, they will find Me and the next move of My Spirit, and they will be judged by My Word in Matthew 25:42-43. *"For I was hungry and you gave Me no meat: I was thirsty and you gave Me no drink: I was a stranger and you took Me not in: naked, and you clothed Me not: sick, and in prison, and you visited Me not."*

Dearest Reader:

I first read this prophecy while I was still in prison. When I did, an explosion went off inside of me! Since then, the Lord told me that the ONE KEY Jesus uses to open up every prison door is THE EXPECTED END! It is what will raise up a Kingdom Army from inside the walls! In March of 2007, a personal word of prophecy was given to me: I WAS TOLD I HAVE AN ARMY!!! Each one of you is a part of this Army! Together we will take the world for Christ!!!

In His Service,

Katie

The Captivity Series: The Key to Your Expected End

Excerpts from the following books are used with permission from the authors and/or publishers:
A Slow and Certain Light by Elisabeth Elliot and *A Purpose Driven Life* by Rick Warren.

Cover concept by **Katie Souza.**

Cover graphics by **iiMAGE** (contact jose@iimageaz.com)

Back cover photo of Katie Souza by **Linda White** (contact lindajft@gmail.com)

EXPECTED END MINISTRIES
PO Box 1289
Maricopa, AZ 85239
623.444.5366
866.790.5090
www.expectedendministries.com

PERSONAL JOURNAL ENTRIES

Author Katie Souza takes Israel's journey in, through and out of prison and directly parallels it to the incarceration experience inmates face today. Throughout the study, Souza continually creates excitement and hope for her readers by interweaving her own miraculous prison story into each teaching.

Four years in the making, *"The Captivity Series the Key to Your Expected End"* is spreading like wild fire through the prison system!

◄ *Ex-felon, Katie Souza, is now Founder and President of Expected End Ministries.*

Testimonies

"... I must say this is probably one of the best and most engaging "Walk With God" books I have read by a contemporary author. It doesn't take all that much imagination for a non-prisoner to apply the principles either. I find myself praising my way through a lot of it, and sometimes there is a "gulp" of conviction, too. " **Terry Northway -God Time Ministries, New Mexico**

"I have read a lot of Christian books by some of the most known Christian Authors and none of them touched and ministered to me the way that your book "The Captivity Series" did...I believe your book had to reach me so that I may have the knowledge I need to reach my Expected End." **Audra R. Israel/ Federal Prison Camp Victorville, California**

"Bravo Katie! The Two million inmates being held captive within our current prison system now have a guidebook to transform the very core of their existence. On behalf of all of them and myself, I thank you." **Star L. Mathias CCA Florence, Arizona**

ISBN: 978-0-9796975-0-0

52000

9 780979 697500